TERROR BY NIGHT

TERROR BY NIGHT

The Official History of the SBS and the Greek Sacred Squadron in the Aegean 1943-1945

Originally compiled from Official Sources and Reports by Observer Officers of No.1 Public Relations Service. M.E.F.

Edited by Alan Ogden

Nine Elms Books

Published in 2017 by Nine Elms Books Ltd

Revised edition 2020

Unit 1G
Clapham North Arts Centre
26–32 Voltaire Road
London SW4 6DH

Email: info@nineelmsbooks.co.uk

nineelmsbooks.co.uk

ISBN: 978-1- 910533-30- 7

Compiled from Official Sources and Reports by Observer Officers of No.1 Public Relations Service. M.E.F. and originally edited by Captain C W Read in 1945 © The National Archive and published under the terms of the Open Government Licence.

Protected by National Archive copyright guidelines and under the terms of the International Copyright Union: all rights reserved. Except for fair use in book reviews, no part of this publication may be reproduced in any form or by any means, electronic
or mechanical, including photocopying, recording or by any information storage or retrieval system without prior permission from the copyright holder.

Introduction and maps copyright © Alan Ogden 2017

Cover illustration reproduced by kind permission of The Imperial War Museum – © Imperial War Museums (Art.IWM ART LD 5197)

Cover design and typesetting by Alex Thornton

Printed in the UK

DEDICATION

This edition of Raiding Forces Aegean [WO 201/2836] is dedicated to the memory of my remarkable cousin, John Lodwick [1916-53], Foreign Legionnaire, S.O.E. operative, S.B.S. officer, and novelist.

Robin Bieber,

London, 2017

Table of Contents

Introduction 1
Preface 3
Statistics 6

PART I Birth of Raiding Forces **9**
Who and Why 13
Attached Troops 16
Diplomacy Fails 25
The Army Moves In and Out 27

PART II Raiders at Work **31**
House Party on Mykonos 32
Death Visits Tilos 36
Reconnaissance on Nisyros 42
Five Headaches on Paros 46
Caiques and Cables 53
Marooned on Kos 58
Party on Symi 62

PART III Bigger and Better Raids **67**
No Escape 75
The Last Shots 83
Alimnia Episode 87
"Parade Dismiss!" 89

We Pay a Debt 98
APPENDIX "A"   "Boarders Away" 100
APPENDIX "B"   Andartes in the Islands 104
APPENDIX "C"   These were the Islands 107
List of Greek Sacred Squadron/Regiment operations in Aegean area
.... 109

Abbreviations

A.A.: Anti-aircraft
E.M.S.: Enemy maritime services
E-boat: German fast motor launch
G.H.Q.: General Headquarters
G.S.R.: Greek Sacred Regiment
H.D.M.L.: Harbour Defence Motor Launch
H.Q.: Headquarters
L.R.D.G.: Long Range Desert group
M.G.: Machine gun
M.L.: Motor Launch
M.M.G.: Medium machine gun
M.T.: Motor Transport
N.A.A.F.I: Navy, Army and Air Force Institute
N.C.O.: Non-commissioned officer
O.R.: Other Ranks
P.O.W.: Prisoner of War
P.T.: Physical Training
Q.M.S.: Quartermaster Sergeant
R.A.C.: Royal Armoured Corps
R.A.F.: Royal Air Force
R.A.M.C.: Royal Army Medical Corps
R.A.S.C.: Royal Army Service Corps
R.E.: Royal Engineers
R.E.M.E.: Royal Mechanical and Electrical Engineers
R.F.: Raiding Forces
R.S.R.: Raiding Support Regiment
S.B.S.: Special Boat Squadron
U.N.R.R.A.: UN Relief and Rehabilitation Administration

Introduction

Raiding Forces Aegean was compiled by Army Public Relations Services in early 1945 and published that July. The date is significant for two reasons.

First, the war with Japan was still raging in the Far East and a number of men from Raiding Forces Aegean were already in or on their way out to South East Asia. So here was a warning to Japanese soldiers who found themselves defending small isolated islands - the SBS is coming to get you! Such was the need for security that names and intimate details of operations had to be restricted.

Secondly, the situation in Greece was deteriorating with a civil war looming on the horizon. The message of Raiding Force Aegean was therefore one of national unity, a story of Greeks along with their English allies fighting the German and Italian occupation armies, not that of Greeks killing fellow Greeks.

The gist of Appendix B is thus all the more surprising in that it is avowedly pro-E.L.A.S., the Communist guerrilla movement which had been responsible for much of the bitter internecine fighting between guerrilla bands in 1943 and 1944 and had then clashed with British liberation forces in Athens. The invective heaped upon Colonel Zervas and E.D.E.S. is a crude smear tactic and has no place in this history.

Although S.O.E.'s Brigadier Barker-Benfield had endorsed E.L.A.S. at the beginning of 1944, subsequent events such as the killing by E.L.A.S. of an S.B.S. officer and outrider and the wounding of a second officer in Crete in January 1945 surely warranted a reappraisal.

Alan Ogden,
London, April 2017.

Preface

This history of Raiding Forces, a unit that for 22 months established a reign of terror and suspense in the hearts of a German Force, a hundred times its number, is necessarily brief.

Details of all 381 raids, attacks and reconnaissances would bore the reader without adding to his knowledge, while other particulars, which might have been added, have been left out after consultation with the Naval and Military Censors, for fear of helping the Japanese.

The founding, training and composition of Raiding Forces are dealt with, it is hoped, in sufficient detail to show what manner of men comprised the patrols, and yet not to fog anyone's mind with technical facts of interest only to the professional staff officer.

The accounts given of various raids show the three phases of Raiding Forces' rising power in the islands and each is typical of a score of others.

The itemised statistics, which follow, show that while the total of Raiding Force casualties was extremely light, the large casualties inflicted on the Axis invaders were out of all proportion to the number of men who caused them. Proof of the gallantry of the troops, who made Raiding Forces famous, is shown by the number of officers and men decorated.

Since this is a military record the magnificent work of the Royal Navy gets little space. It is appropriate, therefore, to mention their work and hazards here.

The vessels the Navy used ranged from Diesel engine caiques to Harbour Defence Motor Launches and Fairmiles. The German "Kriegsmarine" had the advantage of speed, armament, and numbers, and close air support against our ships.

Yet, never was an action refused or lost. With Nelson's famous signal "Engage the enemy more closely" as their motto they drove in to snatch victory in the face of big odds. When needed, they provided supporting fire for the troops ashore, demolished enemy strongpoints and carried military boarding parties to capture the caiques engaged, in the German interest, in moving supplies between the islands.

TERROR BY NIGHT

When the opportunity arose, the Naval Small Craft would make strikes against enemy shipping. On one occasion two little M.L.s hunted a large German cargo vessel and fired over 200 Bofors shells at her as well as a quantity of Oerlikon ammunition. The repeated attack of the two M.L.s eventually drove the damaged ship to seek shelter, although she was escorted by five E-boats, each bigger and more heavily armed than the M.L.s.

But landing, and picking up again, the fighting, demolition and reconnaissance patrols was the chief job of those little ships of the Eastern Mediterranean and they never failed the shore parties.

In the whole period of operations no man was captured and no man's life was lost through the Navy's failure to turn up, in the right place, at the right time.

Taking risks that would horrify a peace-time sailor, they entered bays and channels in the pitch dark, without lights, skirted rocks, reefs and shoals and landed parties on coasts where the enemy was watching for a raid. At all times their work was made harder by the ever present danger of uncharted Axis minefields. Yet no errors in navigation confused the troops as they went ashore, nor was an operation ever delayed except by bad weather.

Much of the morale and daring of the soldiers they carried is reputed to be due to their confidence in the Navy. The certainty of having a ship waiting to take them off after a raid eased the nerve strain of living behind the lines of a cruel and clever army.

When the credit for removing large numbers of men and vast quantities of materials and installations from the Axis service, in a time of vital need, is apportioned, a full half of the credit should go to the officers and men of the Royal Navy.

In carrying Raiding Forces the Navy suffered casualties and damage to vessels, but neither interfered with their concentration on the job in hand and punctuality in picking up and setting down patrols.

The war in the islands was unique, in that neither arms nor armaments played a leading part in the result. It was man against man, where neither press nor radio propaganda could perpetuate the myth of the Nazi "Superman".

PREFACE

In a fight, waged largely at close quarters, determination and a refusal to admit the possibility of defeat were the deciding factors. The British and Greek troops were united as a single fighting entity.

As long as Greece, and the world, remember Thermopylae and Leonidas, King of Sparta and his 300 men who fell there, holding the pass against the Persians, they should remember the 400 men of Raiding Forces.

Substituting Gauleiters for Satraps, the Nazi Dictator followed in the footsteps of Darius and the other autocrats of the Persian empire that ruled the known world before the power of ancient Rome was borne.

Finally, as the Nuremberg Laws and similar Nazi legislation followed the "laws of the Medes and Persian which may not be altered" into the discard of history, so free men, who preferred death to slavery, again freed Greece from a tyrant.

With never more than 400 men available, Raiding Forces created a reign of terror for Nazi and collaborator alike. Everything the Germans could put against our men ranging from the destroyers of the Kriegsmarine to mere booby-traps proved useless against a new "Terror by Night".

Raiding Forces Statistics

Casualties

In their operations British and Greek troops of Raiding Forces inflicted 4,131 known casualties on the enemy, of which over 60% were sustained by the Germans. Other casualties were undoubtedly inflicted, but never made public.

The detailed results are as follows:

Killed	Wounded	Prisoner	Total
288	119	3,724	4,131

During the same period our casualties totalled 93.

These were made up of:-

Killed	Died of wounds	Wounded	Prisoner	Total
16	3	35	39	93

Of these losses 59 were sustained by the Greek and 34 by British personnel.

The contrasted Allied and Axis figures show that Raiding Forces inflicted approximately 47 casualties for every one they sustained. These figures exclude those of the surrendered garrisons in the Dodecanese.

Shipping

The Axis lost 125 ships, totalling approximately 5,000 tons, as a result of raiding activities and in addition to all losses caused by the Royal Navy.

Our own losses by damage, capture or foundering, were four motor launches, four motor torpedo boats, one caique and two dories.

Raids and Reconnaissances

In the period under review British and Greek troops made 381 visits to

RAIDING FORCES STATISTICS

80 different German held islands in the Dodecanese, Aegean, Cyclades and Sporades groups.

Installations

The Axis invaders lost over one million pounds' worth of installations and material as a result of Raiding Forces' activities on the occupied islands.

This figure does not include artillery, machine guns and other weapons destroyed on raids, or captured, nor does it include ammunition, bombs and quarter master's stores of which vast quantities were destroyed or captured.

The main items that come under "installations", which were destroyed by Anglo-Greek attack, are cable and wireless stations, caique building and repair yards, petrol installations, olive oil supplies, fuel pumps, telephone exchanges, harbour installations, signals equipment and maintenance gear.

In a raid on Crete in August 1944 over 300,000 gallons of petrol went up in a long plume of black smoke.

Khios had been raided by an Anglo-Greek Force in June, who damaged the caique building yards and 13 caiques in the water. They also destroyed the cable installation on shore, which was the junction point of all the mainland and inter-island cables, as well as cutting the cables themselves with explosive charges some distance out to sea.

As a result of this attack, the entire system of cable communications was stopped and the Nazis had not been able to get it working again by the time the island was liberated four months later.

Loss of the cable system disorganised inter-communication between the garrisons of the different islands for the remainder of the occupation and threw a great additional strain on the already overloaded wireless service.

In some cases, garrisons were reduced to starting boat services between islands in order to get a form of regular communication, however slow, into working order for their daily needs.

Another loss that had to be faced by the Germans was the cargo in the ships we captured. Wheat and olive oil were the most usual loads, but a "comforts" ship had a quantity of champagne aboard and another vessel a load of Parmesan cheeses, each weighing 100 lbs.

Most mysterious of all the prize cargoes taken was 70 tons of plate glass. Where it had come from, where it was going and what its use could conceivably be, baffled all enquirers.

With neither big stores or fine mansions to use it, on even the biggest islands, there seems to be no chance of making use of it even in peace time.

In the middle of a desperate war, with all the cargo space, in the limited quantity of shipping available needed for urgent priority stores, the mystery of the plate glass becomes even more remarkable.

Royal Marines

One of the outstanding disasters suffered by the German Kriegsmarine was an attack inside Leros harbour, by a small party of the Royal Marine Boom Patrol Detachment, which had been sent from England to join Raiding Forces.

The Marines' objective was to sink two German destroyers and other shipping anchored inside the Leros harbour defences.

The Nazis had taken every precaution for their defence which could occur to the methodical Teuton mind. Guards, motor boat patrols, searchlights sweeping the surface of the water and boom defences were all part of an elaborate protection scheme.

In spite of this, the Marines arrived in their tiny Folboats, attached explosive charges, under water, to the two destroyers and two cargo vessels and retired the way they had come.

Both vessels were so badly damaged in the explosions that followed that they had to be towed to the Piraeus, in Greece, for extensive repairs and were in dock for three months after that.

The other two of the four German destroyers in Greek waters at that time were equally unlucky. One of them was sunk by the R.A.F., while the other was sunk by a submarine.

PART I
The Birth of the Raiding Forces

On 9th September 1943, a party of fifty men of the Special Boat Service, one of the units whose very existence was kept secret, landed on the tiny Dodecanese island of Kastellorizo, just off the Turkish coast, overcame the slight resistance of the garrison of 300 Italians in strongly fortified positions, protected by artillery, and captured the island, later to be known under the code name of "Trombone" as a headquarters for further operations.

This daring operation, made by specially trained men and completely unexpected by the enemy, was the opening move in a scientifically planned campaign to tie down large numbers of German troops where they could not be used to reinforce those attempting to stem the Allied landings in Italy at Salerno and Reggio.

In addition, this threat to the vulnerable flank made any thought of pushing East through the Levant to the oil wells of Iraq and Iran impossible, unless these raiders were eliminated once and for all.

Finally, it menaced the strategic Axis base on Crete. With British Forces operating across the rear lines, supply was likely to become a headache.

* * *

The capture of Kastellorizo marks the birth of Raiding Forces in the Aegean and the start of a campaign that immobilised 40,000 German troops in defence of the Dodecanese, Aegean, Cyclades and Sporades groups of islands as well as the two main bastions of Crete and Rhodes.

To make up Raiding Forces a number of small, specialist units whose battle experience had been gained in the desert, often far behind the Germans lines, were grouped together.

These units were (1) the Special Boat Service, who in addition to being experts in the collapsible Folboat and other small craft, were all trained parachutists, (2) the Long Range Desert Group, the story of whose exploits raiding Axis airfields and rear area installations by jeep from their hideout in one of the southern Oases, was a closely kept G.H.Q. secret. On joining Raiding Forces, however, the Long Range Desert Group added parachuting to their other skills. (3) The Holding Unit, Special Forces, through which came a number of experienced officers and men from the Malta Commando after the siege of that island was raised. (4) The Greek Sacred Squadron formed in the previous year entirely of officers of the Royal Hellenic Army who had escaped, after the invasion of Greece, to continue the fight. They were the third revival of this famous unit, only formed in time of Greece's greatest danger.

The first squadron had died to a man, resisting the Spartans at Thebes in 370 B.C., the second was wiped out fighting for the freedom of Greece in 1821, against the Turks. The third squadron has conquered and returns home in glory.

(5), The Kalpaks. A less gently mannered age than this would have called these enthusiasts thugs; we politely say they showed a marked disregard for the sanctity of human life.

The different units all came under H.Q. Raiding Forces, which consisted of a small number of staff officers, with the minimum O.R. personnel, Signals, Royal Engineers, R.E.M.E., and P.T. Staff, the whole being under the Commander, Raiding Forces, Brigadier (then Colonel) D.J.T. Turnbull, CBE, DSO.

In November 1944, just after the unfortunate Aegean Force had been driven from its toe-hold on Kos and Leros, a further unit was formed for Raiding Forces and known as the Raiding Support Regiment, it comprised five batteries of parachutists manning supporting weapons.

The final addition to the combined strength was in the early summer of 1944 when a Royal Marine Boom Patrol Detachment was sent from England.

Raiding Forces was a blend of the nations for, in addition to men from the United Kingdom, Greece and Turkey, there were a number of South Africans in the R.S.R., and a whole squadron of New Zealanders in the L.R.D.G. The United States were represented by a number of men of the American Field Service who resigned from their unit to enlist as Parachutists in the S.B.S. (the rank is equivalent to private in the

THE BIRTH OF THE RAIDING FORCES

Infantry). These American volunteers served as Medical Orderlies and showed extreme bravery on operations. One won a Military Medal and one a George Medal.

United by the comradeship, which is formed by taking a parachute course together, and the reliance engendered by sharing the hazards of many operations, each Detachment and Section of Raiding Forces has been remarkable for the way in which officers and men had got together in a friendship which far from undermining discipline has rather buttressed it.

This is particularly noteworthy when it is remembered that the quarters for officers and men, between raids, were both cramped and Spartan. They lived together in overcrowded caiques with no amenities, their only forms of sport and exercise being swimming and rock-climbing.

Yet this was the unit whose swift success, despite the disparity in numbers was to become the pattern of a new and highly successful Allied offensive in the Aegean, at a time when German air-borne troops, supported by sea landings had just inflicted a noteworthy defeat on us there, and had cost us severe casualties, particularly in prisoners.

* * *

When it was known that Italy was likely to come over to the Allies, it was decided to make an effort to persuade the Italians in the Dodecanese to resist German occupation, hand over control of the islands to us and, in fact, thwart the Germans generally.

It was quite obvious that if Italy did leave the Axis, the Germans would at once secure any points then held by the Italians with their own troops. Part of the allied intention was to forestall this.

However, the plan failed which might have given us control of the Dodecanese and almost succeeded in bringing them to us without bloodshed. That it failed was because the Italian Admiral was more afraid of the Nazis than of Britain.

Thanks to the unorthodox character of the Allied campaign in this part of the Mediterranean, our scheme was flexible enough to develop as the situation changed. When the attempt to persuade the Italian to our side had failed, the alternative course of setting up a reign of terror for the German garrisons on the Greek islands was applied and within a few months the war of nerves was in full swing.

Those who survived, including the thousands who were ultimately taken off Rhodes and Crete as prisoners of war, will remember all their lives the haunting threat that each night brought. The silent approach of death by knife, bullet and grenade from men who never slept, had undermined their morale and set up an almost constant state of fear. The menace of these men who came, none knew how, or from where, who blew up radio stations, wiped out strongpoints, spirited away individuals who had betrayed Allied agents, and left time bombs in the beds of German commanders, was a shadow that never left the garrisons and in time filled the hospitals with nerve cases.

On top of all this, the destruction of shipping made them feel that the dangers involved in leaving the islands were almost as great as those in staying.

In short, havoc was made of German plans by a mysterious and sinister force that almost seemed to get off lightly, leaving fantastically disproportionate numbers of casualties among the Axis garrison.

Who and Why

As a result of security precautions, which have undoubtedly saved many lives, very few men and women, even in the services, have a clear idea of either the function of Raiding Forces, or how it differs from other superficially similar units such as the Commandos or Army Parachute Battalions.

Probably the simplest way to avoid confusion is to describe briefly the functions of each, without going into too much detail. Basically, an Army Parachute Battalion is a normal infantry battalion that is transported to the scene of the action by aeroplane and parachute, in a precisely parallel fashion to the way mechanised infantry are carried to their battle ground by lorry.

Admittedly there are more stringent medical examinations and age requirements before admission to parachute battalions, but the men are, to all intents and purposes, specially trained infantrymen, armed with infantry weapons.

Commandos, on the other hand, are specially trained shock troops. They are put in to do a certain job, which they must complete however great their casualties. Commandos are in fact expendable and the rule guiding their employment is largely "Is this operation worth the number of casualties it will cost?" Commando raids are, by their very nature, expensive, but, providing the agreed ratio of casualties to the complete job is not exceeded, the operation is deemed a success.

In Raiding Forces entirely the reverse applies. Every single casualty, killed, wounded or missing decreases the percentage of completeness in a success. Only the operation in which loss is inflicted on the enemy with no casualties to our side is considered a 100% job and patrol leaders have orders to withdraw rather than incur avoidable losses of men.

The reasoning behind this is quite simple. The men of Raiding Forces cost a lot of money and time to train and facilities for producing first class work are limited. You cannot indent on a reinforcement depot for men to fill the gaps in the ranks caused by an unlucky venture.

The work too demands a special type of man and only a percentage of the soldiers in the required age and medical categories are suitable. Over and above the physical qualities required to carry an 80lb rucksack on a 20 mile forced march along mountain water courses and goat tracks, he needs certain special factors which are born in him and cannot be acquired.

One of the most important of these is resistance to boredom. The man must be able to keep himself amused from the resources of his own mind for two or three weeks on end under conditions where more than a whispered phase of conversation is barred and no books are available.

Another is the capacity to do without privacy for months on end, to be keen and alert under conditions where he is cooped up in a tiny ship with the same comrades for long stretches and cannot get away from them for so much as a minute.

Ability to ignore fatigue, and do without food, water, or sleep can be acquired. The ability to hear the man in the next bunk continually sucking his tooth, without losing either temper, or good humour, is only born in a man.

Of such are the personnel of Raiding Forces made, but even some of those fall out, usually due to an inability to absorb tuition accurately enough, or fast enough. A moment's mistake in calculation on a demolition, or an error due to having forgotten the formula and having to guess, may cost the unit a whole patrol. If there is even the possibility that this may happen the man goes back to his unit.

After this the training starts. First the parachute course where he does six jumps by day and one by night at continually decreasing altitudes, after a ground course designed to prepare the right muscles for jumping, teach him the theory of parachuting and give him confidence in his equipment.

Serious accidents are a negligible percentage and less than one in a hundred refuse to jump.

After this comes a course in mountain warfare followed by snow and ski training. From land to water is the next stage and he learns the handling and navigation of small boats followed by a course on under-

WHO AND WHY

water work and the use of the Davis escape apparatus. It is assumed that he is a strong and confident swimmer before he starts training.

After this is a period spent on the care, handling and use of explosives followed by practical demolitions. Then his knowledge of our own weapons must be brought up to the minute and the skilled use of all kinds of mortars, machine guns and small arms become instinctive.

Finally, he must acquire an equally exhaustive knowledge of all enemy weapons. After a period of test and rehearsal he will then be allowed to take part in raids.

As assessment of the cost, in time and specialist instructors alone is sufficient to show why Raiding Force personnel are not expendable. Heavy casualties in one operation may prevent an even more important one being carried out because of a shortage of men.

This knowledge of the type of man employed and the type of training he received should explain why Raiding Forces made impossible operations look feasible and then carried them out with success.

Attached Troops

Apart from the trained parachutists who made up the main body of troops, both British and Greek, in the unit there were many specialists "attached".

In actual fact, the attached troops were as much part of Brigadier Turnbull's command as any of the men originally posted to him from the S.B.S., or L.R.D.G. For the men of the Royal Engineers, R.E.M.E, Signals and R.A.M.C., with Raiding Forces any distinction that might exist was purely on paper.

When it came to training or exercises, they did precisely the same as the rest of the troops. They parachuted, sailed, marched on mountains or in snow, and either fulfilled the rigorous training schedule, or were sent back to their units. There were no vacancies for passengers and the unqualified men messed the boat – and ultimately the raids.

Royal Corps of Signals

The largest body of attached troops were the Raiding Force Signals, who also carried the heaviest burden in the Aegean patrols. Literally

ATTACHED TROOPS

they had to pass their training tests twice over, first when, as members of the Royal Corps of Signals, they proved themselves first class radio operations, able to work under heavy fire and the worst conditions.

Their second set of tests came from Raiding Forces, who made sure they were tested and qualified raiders, before they would even consider their qualifications as Signals experts.

These men were the cream of a proud corps, both in skill and physical fitness. All of them were volunteers and, in the view of the Commander, Raiding Forces, contributed a most vital share in the success of every operation.

At the farewell parade and inspection of Raiding Forces, General Sir Bernard Paget, the Commander-in-Chief, Middle East Forces, marked them out for the praise in a speech in which he congratulated all men of Raiding Forces in the highest terms.

"I wish to make special mention of Raiding Force Signals... they have done splendid work" was the keynote of the C-in-C's remarks about them.

When a patrol sets out on a raid each man carries all his own kit. Not only his arms, ammunition, grenades and any spare clothing and bedding he may take must be carried, but also in his rucksack are his rations, the only food he will eat for a possible 14 or 21 days' patrol. No food can be obtained from the islands raided.

In addition to this weighty load, the two Signalmen attached to each patrol carry a wireless transmitting and receiving set with two heavy accumulators to provide the power. Although carrying this additional burden they never cause the pace of the patrol to be slackened on even the steepest climbs or the roughest water course or goat track.

Then, when the rest of the patrol, except the sentries, are relaxing they must keep on the alert to listen at the routine times when a message may be sent to them, decode it and pass it to the patrol commander.

Twice a day they must convert his reports into an unbreakable cipher and transmit it to the powerful receiving station at R.F. rear H.Q., in Egypt. It is from there that the message goes back to their own operational H.Q., for the raiding sets are of secret design, to make listening hard on all but certain, special sets and to give enemy Direction Finding stations little chance to plot their location on the map.

On one occasion one of our fighting patrols reached an impasse on Naxos. The enemy was clever enough to get them in a position from which they could neither go forward to the attack nor withdraw without heavy loss.

An emergency call by the patrol signalmen to G.H.Q., reported the situation, gave location and other details and asked for help from the air. No time was wasted in relaying the message to the R.A.F. and in a short while Beaufighters based on Egypt, had located the patrol and obliterated the Axis obstacles to their complete success, although there was no possible landing ground nearer than their base, over 400 miles away, except those controlled by the Nazis.

As the vital, and only, link between the men in action and the Raiding Force staff, who alone can provide assistance and support when things look grim, or an opportunity arises to turn a local success into victory, the Signals responsibility is heavy, but they carry it as lightly as the overweight packs they take on patrols.

R.E.M.E. Goes to Sea

The gloating Light Repair Section of R.E.M.E. attached to Raiding Forces also received special commendation from the Commander-in-Chief at the farewell parade. To some people, it may sound a paradox that a unit, without motor transport when on operations, needs a R.E.M.E. detachment and keeps it at sea in a caique.

Yet these craftsmen are among the busiest specialists in Raiding Forces, their specialised skill making up for the few of them who went to the Aegean.

First of their tasks is keeping the arms of the raiders in perfect order. At sea, the atmosphere conspires to corrode and ruin the sub-machine guns, automatic carbines and other weapons of a patrol. When they land, rocks, and the rough terrain of the islands cause numerous types of damage that need specialist repair and range from the telescope of a sniper's rifle knocked out of alignment on a rock to the mechanism of a Vickers stuck and sanded up as a result of a near miss by an Axis mortar bomb.

ATTACHED TROOPS

Damaged weapons cannot be evacuated to a well-equipped static base for repair. What cannot be put right by skill, and the equipment R.E.M.E. can carry on a caique crowded with troops, must be left undone and the weapon unserviceable for the rest of the detachment's tour of duty.

Instead of putting patches on the burst inner tubes of M.T. they repair and make watertight the tears, caused by night landings on a rocky shore and enemy action, in the fragile Folboats of the unit.

Another responsibility is the maintenance of the petrol motors and charging plant which provide electricity for the wireless batteries of signals. Dory motors too, although of sturdy marine construction, develop mysterious faults that take hours to detect and repair.

Their intelligence, as well as trade skill, is exercised when they are at sea, far from the base. Since its inception, Raiding Forces have used certain types of Axis weapons in making life difficult for their previous owners.

Spares can be only obtained by stripping down some weapons to their component parts in order to rebuild the rest, or making the required part out of faith and scrap. So often has this miracle been performed that R.E.M.E no longer get credit for it.

In action their most urgent job is to be able instantly to repair an enemy weapon they have never previously seen, so that it may be used again against the man who, a few minutes previously, aimed it at us.

In rest periods between patrols the R.E.M.E. personnel get no rest. Out comes the old gramophone with a broken spring, the Primus stove in the last stages of senile decay and a host of other objects. The flattery in the remark "It's easy for you" bounces off unheeded. Their job is to maintain and repair everything in sight and they do it.

After one operation, while waiting to be taken off by the Navy, a Craftsman was asked why he did not mend the large tear in the sea of his trousers. "Well sir" he told the officer, "I dinna think the hole is in sight to be repaired" and, as an afterthought he added, "Forbye, Sir, there's not a man in the patrol has a needle and cotton with him."

The Royal Engineers were there

Sappers from the Royal Engineers, with their usual nonchalant, but respectful handling of explosives, were attached to Raiding Forces from the start for special work.

Although every man on a raid carried his share of demolition explosives and had qualified to use them on a training course and in action, no detachment could do without its personal sapper team.

Instinctively they knew the minimum charge needed for any demolition and the exact spot to place it for the maximum affect. But their greatest value was that they could gap a minefield, clear booby traps and make safe an enemy demolition charge in the middle of an action.

The majority of them were well above the average age of the rest of the raiders, and they appeared to have shed their nerves with their milk teeth. To see one of these sappers advance against enemy fire was an education in coolness.

On his back was a rucksack, filled with prepared charges, time pencils, instantaneous detonation fuse, primers, igniters and detonators. At the front of his equipment the Bren pouches bulged with charges of mixed plastic explosive and thermite. Yet his main concern, as he advanced through the screen of tracer and incendiary bullets, whose touch would have set off his load of explosives, was to find a target for his sub-machine gun.

That same talent for improvisation, either in attack or defence, that spread the praises of the Royal Engineers all over India, in the days of John Company, has not deserted the Corps today. Their sappers with Raiding Forces have shown that, to them, no task is impossible, and given the simplest of equipment have operated in such a way as almost to make the Nazis believe in fairies.

Mysterious demolitions set by the R.E., were done in such a way as to make the enemy think that no man could have by-passed all the defences, laid a charge and gone without leaving a clue.

The combination of rigid security coupled with false clues and deliberate mystification of the enemy served to baffle the Nazi intelligence right through the Aegean campaign.

ATTACHED TROOPS

* * *

How Raiding Force patrols arrived, and left, and the points from which they did it, remained a secret all through the 22-month terror. It is still kept today because other units will doubtless find it useful in liquidating the yellow Nazis of the Far East.

Out of their final total of 381 raids the reconnaissances made the patrols were ambushed on only two occasions by the enemy they so relentlessly harassed.

It was finally decided that these two serious reverses were not mere chance but the result of a leakage of information. In the first case 40 men of the Greek Sacred Regiment were ambushed on Samos in May 1944, and had to scatter to escape, leaving their operational tasks undone.

When the Navy arrived at the rendezvous to pick up the party, only five men were waiting. During the next three weeks, further pick-up points were arranged, for various times, and communicated by Army secret agents to Greek civilians on the island, whose loyalty and discretion were known.

These men could be relied on to tell any of the missing patrol, who were alive and free, and make certain they were not going to be trapped as they made their get-away.

On these trips 30 men were picked up in small bodies by the waiting Navy and in the finish only five men failed to escape. Death, or serious wounds had made the Navy's gesture useless to them.

Is there a doctor in the force?

Perfect physical fitness and abundant self-confidence made the Raiders on patrol feel no sense of worry because they had no medical officer with them for emergencies. Casualties were few, and the R.A.M.C. sergeant and his medical orderlies, including the volunteers from the American Field Service dealt efficiently with the odd gunshot wound or accident.

The one and only Medical Officer in the unit had a very busy time because often he had to choose between which of our or five Raiding parties he would accompany. It was only when all personnel were going on the same operation that he could be confident that no one would be overlooked.

Casualties on the Simi raid were light on the Allied side. Only one British Officer, two Greek Officers and three other ranks were wounded, while the total of Axis wounded was small, but provided plenty of work for a doctor who had only one skilled orderly to do everything.

However, if the men of Raiding Forces had little need of a doctor, the people of the islands they visited had plenty. Malnutrition over the years of occupation had lowered these once hardy people's resistance to disease, while practically all the drugs and medicines had been used.

As the patrols and detachments pressed forward their attacks and liberated island after island, the doctor found his regimental aid post becoming a civilian clinic in the absence of battle casualties. Sometimes he was able to contact a local Greek doctor and provide him with a small supply of drugs and medicines for his patients.

Since the Germans and Italians had stopped the import of any drugs, or medicines, for civilians more than two years previously, even the smallest quantity of medical supplies meant a big alleviation of the suffering caused by Axis callousness to the sufferings of the civil population.

As well as starting a friendly relationship with the island medical men, the Raiding Force doctor and his R.A.M.C. staff were able to investigate various civil health records and public sanitation problems that produced information of a great importance later.

Liberation

The success of the Raiding Forces policy led to the Germans evacuating the Aegean before they started to withdraw from the Greek mainland. This created a situation which had not been foreseen when the Allied Military Liaison scheme for temporary administration of the country was drawn up.

With the liberation of each fresh island the civil relief needs increased enormously. The German technique of requisitioning much of the local food supply and prohibiting imports from outside produced a situation which the Nazi habit of looting homes and the complete absence of clothing supplies rendered desperate.

The grim undernourishment of the civil population, the almost complete absence of soap and disinfectants and the ragged clothing which men, women and children alike wore because replacement was impossible, made the immediate outbreak of typhus or an equally grim epidemic disease probable at any time.

To re-draw the Allied Military Liaison scheme to cover this emergency was impossible in the time available. An "ad hoc" scheme had to be improvised at once and put into immediate action.

To achieve results without delay, Nos. 4 and 4 districts of Allied Military Liaison (Greece) were put under the authority of the Commander, Raiding Forces, the combined unit being given the new name of Force 142. This organisation worked excellently and continued in operation until the Force Commander handed over his civilian relief responsibilities to U.N.R.R.A. in June 1945, and both British and Greek personnel of Raiding Forces returned to Egypt and prepared to disband.

The problems of civil administration, in the territory than his men had wrestled from the Nazis, were numerous, but the experiences of the past year made them easier to overcome.

Ever since the dark days of defeat in which the first operations in the Aegean were carried out and the main part of Raiding Forces was perfecting itself for the new role in an orgy of training near Haifa in Palestine, Brigadier Turnbull had been accustomed to working on the move with only a tiny staff to aid him.

Moving continuously by land, sea and air between the Naval Base at Alexandria, G.H.Q., Palestine and the forward base of his men in the Aegean, he managed to eliminate much of the paper work and simplify the staff direction of operations to an enormous degree.

Emphasis was still placed on detailed planning, the absorption of all possible information from the R.A.F.'s photo reconnaissance pictures, exact written orders and the use of all reliable local guides, but the paper war was liquidated.

Statements, returns, proformas and all the repetitive time-wasting documents that provide so little of value for the time wasted in compilation had been cut out. No one complained because the staff was so small that junior officers had to work all the time. There were none of the staff captains whose sole reason for existence is compiling unread summaries from unreadable returns.

The approach to civil administration and all its problems was made refreshingly simple by Brigadier Turnbull's regime. Orders were given direct to the men who would carry them out; the departmental minute which passed the responsibility on to other shoulders vanished.

Ensuring that only the man who was to do the job got the order gave the Force Commander time to help the Greek Civil Commissioners and straighten out the complex problems of civil relief and rehabilitation. As well as doing this he watched the political situation closely and the manifold changes that occurred as the Germans retreated.

Raiding Forces carried on with their operations. The Brigadier found time from his many jobs to increase the tempo of operations. Soon a period of bigger and better raids started dwarfing the ambitious operations of the pre-liberation period.

Diplomacy fails

On the eve of the Armistice with Italy [1] Brigadier Turnbull, with a small number of officers, was rushed to the Aegean by aeroplane and high speed launch.

His mission was to attempt to land on Rhodes and persuade Admiral Campioni, the Italian Commander, to resist the Germans and hand over the Dodecanese Islands to the Allied Forces.

Such a decision would create many difficulties and supply problems for the German garrison on Crete; it would also lessen the strategic value of that island as a threat to our North African conquests, the oil pipe line ports and the Levant route to the oilfields of Iraq and Iran.

Two of Brigadier Turnbull's officers, Major Lord Jellicoe and Major Dolby, were dropped on Rhodes by parachute in an attempt to see the Admiral and get him to agree to a meeting and discussion with the Brigadier.

The parachute jump was no picnic as both officers received a very hot reception from the island's garrison as they came down. Although fired on by every available weapon from anti-aircraft guns to rifles, neither of them was hit. Unfortunately, Major Dolby broke his leg in landing.

Major Jellicoe and he decided their best course was to let themselves be captured and then demand an interview with Admiral Campioni. If he would see them they would have a chance to state their case, while if he refused they would be no worse off than if they had not surrendered, for a hunted man has little chance of interviewing a reluctant island commander who is taking no chances.

Their plan worked and shortly after they had been taken prisoner Admiral Campioni agreed to receive them and grant an interview.

While Major Jellicoe and Major Dolby were parachuting to earth in a cloud of shell fragments and bullets, a captured Italian seaplane was flying without lights past the north-eastern tip of Rhodes.

On board was Brigadier Turnbull bound for Simi, a small island off

1 7 September 1943

the Turkish coast some 20 miles north west of Rhodes, where he had planned to wait until the Italian Admiral would discuss matters with him.

The remaining officers were on board a high-speed launch which stood off Rhodes Harbour to await events.

When the two parachutists were taken before the Italian Admiral they saw a frightened old man, terrified of the possibility that the Germans would learn that a British Mission had visited him.

Fighting had already broken out on the island between the Germans and Italian units who wanted to follow the action of their mother country and surrender the islands to the victorious allies who had already landed at Reggio in the south of Italy and were then forcing a beachhead at Salerno further to the north.

Admiral Campioni had made his mind up with the obstinacy of the weak. He refused even to meet Brigadier Turnbull, let alone discuss any question of surrender with him. His duty and his inclination lay to his country's former allies, the Nazis.

Already, he pointed out, the Germans had dealt with the Italian units on Rhodes who had been foolish enough to want to extend the armistice at home to this outpost. He also inferred that he had no enthusiasm for martyrdom and that he could take a hint as well as the next man, when it was rubbed in by the Nazis' treatment of Italians who wanted to surrender.

The interview ended on a note of urgency. Admiral Campioni pointed out that he had risked his life in seeing Major Jellicoe and Major Dolby and that he was taking no more chances. As it was he would probably be shot if news of the interview reached the Gestapo, even though he had refused their request.

This was his last word and the two British officers were bundled off Rhodes in a hurry, less than 24 hours after they had dropped in to interview the Admiral.

The Army Moves In – and Out

Since the Italians refused the peace offer, only one course was left to the Allies – the Italians must be compelled to surrender. Invasion and capture of the key islands was the only form of compulsion the Axis understood.

The initiative had already been taken by the S.B.S., who landed on Kos while Brigadier Turnbull and the L.R.D.G. landed in Leros. A little while later they were followed by a company and a half of parachutists from the 11th Battalion, the Parachute Regiment, under Major George Gilchrist, who came down on Kos to be well received by the Italians who no longer wanted to fight, after having seen the S.B.S. The nearest approach to a battle at this stage was when a small party of British parachute other ranks invaded the Italian Garrison Officers' Club, drank a bottle of the best champagne each and marched out again, before their horrified and unwilling Italian hosts could even ask them to pay for their drinks.

Meanwhile several thousand British infantrymen were moving in by sea, escorted by the Free French and British Navies. With the infantry, most of whom had undergone three years of siege in Malta before going to Egypt a few months before, were Field and A.A. detachments, sappers, signals, R.A.S.C. and all the other ancillary units that a force in the field has; even a N.A.A.F.I. went with them.

Not the least imposing of these ancillary troops were a number of staff officers, many of them elderly. They were the Military-Governors-to-be and would take over the administration of the islands as they fell into Allied hands.

Spearheading the landings, as advance guard, were the newly-formed Raiding Forces detachments. The two important islands of Kos and Leros were taken over without opposition, the majority of the Italian Garrisons coming over to the Allied side and continuing with their duty. Among these Italian units were the coast defence artillerymen.

Several minor islands also fell into Allied hands, while Colonel Tsigantes and the Greek Sacred Squadron which he commanded were dropped on Samos, which was of great strategic value.

The Sacred Squadron acquired by this the honour of being the first component unit in the newly formed Raiding Forces to jump into action, an example the newly trained parachutists of the L.R.D.G and S.B.S. were eager to imitate.

Raiding Forces personnel stayed during the period of uneasy calm on Kos and Leros, although the Greeks remained on Samos. A German attempt to recapture the islands was thought to be inevitable but the garrison were satisfied they could repel it.

The Nazis struck at dawn on Sunday, October 3rd, with a combined airborne and sea attack. Optimistic bulletins were issued about driving the invaders back into the sea, but the fact that the Italian gunners had been given no practice in firing live ammunition, because of an economy policy of the Italian home government, turned the scales in the Nazis' favour.

While the British Infantry put up a stubborn fight against parachutists supported by dive bombers in the interior of the island the sea-borne invasion, although suffering losses, sailed through the barrage of ill-aimed shells from the Italian gunners and established their beach head.

Many of the Italians paid for their poor shooting with their lives.

Six days after their first landing all Kos was in German hands. More time passed and on November 12th the Nazis launched their attack on Leros and soon cut the island in two. The British garrison resisted gallantly until November 16th when the island capitulated.

During all this confused period Raiding Force patrols were active on these islands, operating from bases established at Simi and Kalymnos.

Major (now Lt-Col) Jellicoe was on Leros during the negotiations for surrender. His jeep was a familiar sight all over the island and he seemed to bear a charmed life.

When he arrived for the last conference, Major Jellicoe discovered that surrender had not only been decided on, but was actually being carried out.

German sentries with sub-machine guns patrolled the British H.Q., while others rounded up the British troops in temporary P.O.W. cages.

THE ARMY MOVES IN – AND OUT

While he was scheming to get away, a German officer ordered him to join a party of officers from the British staff who were being marched off.

With a flash of inspiration Major Jellicoe told the Nazi that his troops had received no orders to surrender and would fight on unless he went back and gave them instructions. Armed with a pass to get him through the German control points he raced across the island in his jeep, reached the patrol and ultimately organised the escape of not only the S.B.S. and L.R.D.G. personnel but also a number of other troops who had evaded the P.O.W. net.

PART II

Raiders at Work

Aegean islands are very individual in character, although they are all larger or smaller peaks and portions of the same submarine plateau that rises from the bottom of the sea. As a result, the raids on the various islands although similar in objectives, resulted in quite different kinds of stories in the reports made by the officer or N.C.O. in charge of a party on his return.

Nevertheless, there is a sameness about the work as a whole so that it is not possible to include an account of everything Raiding Forces did, although each official report is lit up with vivid flashes of incidents graphically told.

In this necessarily brief record a selection has been made of different types of raid, made as the campaign progressed, to try to illustrate the general style of the work through particular incidents. My object has been to strike a balance between including too much detail on the one hand and, on the other, a bald story that would cover the whole ground, without the real interest. The following narratives, therefore, are a few that necessarily omit by far the greater part of the experiences members of the force will recall with vividness or pride; but they give the reader an aside picture typical of how the job was done. But remember there were, in all, 381 of these raids, each with its quota of nervous strain and moments of tense anxiety when it looked as if the greatly numerical masses of the Germans would wipe out the tiny patrol – but the motto of Raiding Forces is "Who Dares Wins".

House Party on Mykonos

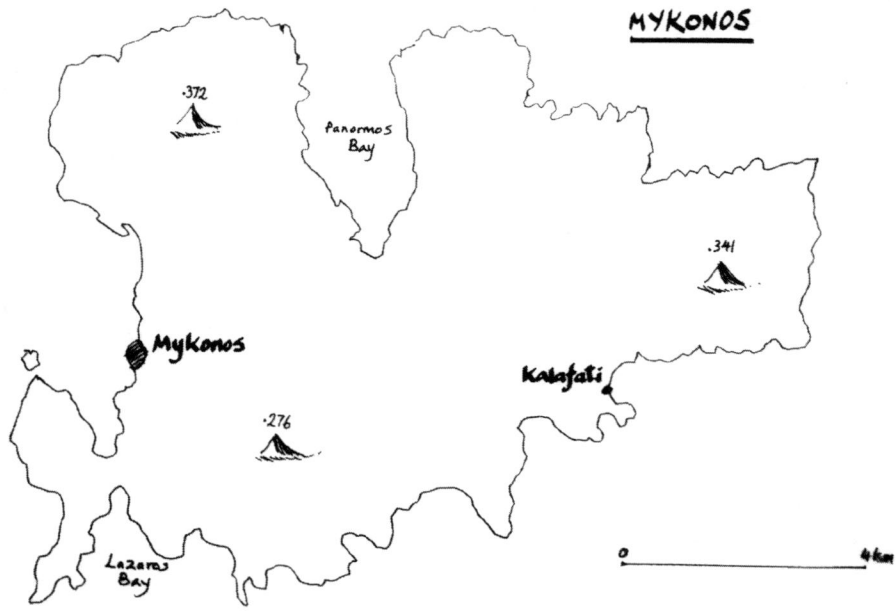

"Nearly everybody on the island knew of our presence – except the Germans," said Lt Lodwick. "They were taken completely unawares when we came to attack them."

The island was Mykonos, and the attack became a siege of the principal house, garrisoned by Germans – "and a pretty deadly house party it turned out to be," as one member of the patrol of ten put it.

Led by Lt. Lodwick, the party had landed in Lazaretto Bay on Mykonos at 22.30 hours, 22nd April. The object was purely to recce the island, in particular the areas occupied by Germans, with a view to subsequent operations on a large scale.

They forced the door of a disused hut, and lay up there during the night. But when dawn broke it became evident that it would be impossible to conceal their presence from the islanders. The whole island was studded with houses and smallholdings.

HOUSE PARTY ON MYKONOS

So Lt. Lodwick took the bold course of frankly enlisting the co-operation of the inhabitants. The patrol pooled all the food and rations they could spare, and distributed it to the islanders they met.

Some of the Greeks went into the town and returned with all the available information about the Germans. When it was pieced together it was established that there were eight Germans on Mykonos – six in a house by the town, under a Sergeant, and two in a lighthouse.

It was decided to attack the house at dawn, and deal with the other Germans afterwards.

At daybreak, the patrol was in position, and the first shot killed the German sergeant who was on the balcony. The enemy tumbled out of bed to meet the onrush, and threw grenades down the stairs, wounding Lt. Lodwick. While his men fired at all the windows, he called on the Germans to surrender.

They lay doggo and refused to make any reply. Meanwhile, Pte Perkins had neutralised their W/T room. The Germans were cut off, and the attack had become a siege.

By now, the whole party had taken cover and were firing at the windows – making sorties as far as the house as often as they could. Cpl Conby, Cpl D'Arcy, and Pte Jarrell several times fought their way into the house. Pte Jarrell captured a Schmeisser when the Germans were forced to vacate the ground floor. But the enemy defence was determined throughout.

Cpl Conby, already injured in the face and hands, was hit in the thigh by a German grenade, but in spite of his wounds he went back on a mule to get fresh ammunition.

The whole party were determined to get that house and the Germans in it. Then a new factor entered the situation. Planes were heard, droning across the sky, and they were almost overhead – six Junkers 88, which must have been escorting a convoy through the Mykoni Channel.

The besieged Germans promptly started firing Verey lights. Pte Hancock and Pte Creevy manoeuvred into a good position and settled down to stop this with their Brens. And it was at this point that the major of the island arrived. Instructed by Lt. Lodwick, he sheltered behind the garden wall, and called out to the Germans to surrender.

"Tell them that if they don't surrender," Lt. Lodwick said, "they will be burnt to death with petrol."

At the same time, the patrol leader arranged for thirty Greeks to go to the mayor's house where petrol was stored in drums, and bring it back to the house. The plan was to roll it against the walls, and set the whole place in flames.

The startled Germans realised only too well how easily this could be done. And if anything more was needed to convince them, they had it when Greek guerrillas arrived with a German prisoner taken on the road to the lighthouse.

The prisoner called out to his comrades that they had just five minutes to live unless they came out of the house with their hands up.

For a few seconds there was silence. Then they came tumbling out of the house to give themselves up. The siege had lasted four hours, and when the German planes came over it had looked as though our men might have to abandon their quarry.

No sooner had the Germans surrendered than about 500 Greeks invaded the house, and stripped it of all its food supplies.

It caused the raiding force some difficulty in concluding their job, which was to collect all the German papers and documents in the building. But this was done, and they were able to relax for a moment.

They fortified themselves with a light lunch in the hotel of the nearby town, and then returned on mule-back to the shore. Greek guerrillas had been sent out to collect the second German from the lighthouse. He was found in the middle of the road hopefully firing Verey lights, and was escorted back to base by Cpl D'Arcy and Pte Jarrell, who had gone along to see him safely into custody.

At 20.40 hours on 24th April, the party sailed from Mykonos, taking their prisoners with them – seven altogether. Other captured items included weapons, the documents, wireless code books, and 6,000 gallons of petrol. The petrol was distributed amongst the Greeks who had already put to good use the entire store of food in the German H.Q.

"Given time and isolation," said the sober and matter-of-fact report on this patrol, "they will always surrender."[1]

[1] Mykonos was later liberated by the G.S.R. in September 1944

Death Visits Tilos

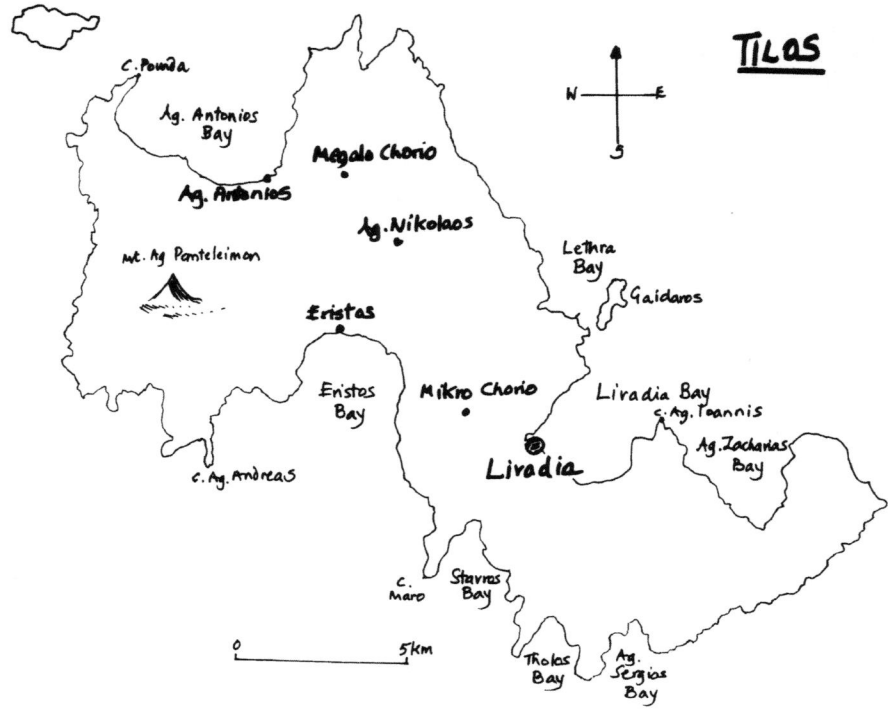

The road on the island of Tilos in April 1944, by a patrol of 10 men gives the tempo of all these operations. An American war correspondence accompanied the party, and seems to have enjoyed himself; he distinguished himself among the raiders by wearing a tie throughout the incident.

The party consisted of a lieutenant, two corporals and six men of Raiding Forces, and a junior Greek officer. Their orders were to attack shipping, to attack an isolated enemy detachment in a definite area of the island, to take prisoners and attack "targets of opportunity". Here are excerpts from the laconic report made after the raid:

"We were landed from a small naval motor launch at 00.45 hours, 9th April; …. Corporal Hughes and Parachutist Williams left by Folboat at 01.30 hours for Cape Aghios Ioannis area, with orders to return on

DEATH VISITS TILOS

D-plus-3 night (see separate report)."

This brief note is strictly military. It says nothing of letting a dinghy down the side of the ship just after midnight and rowing quietly up to the beach, possibly mined and, if information had leaked, possibly ambushed.

After the first half dozen experiences of this kind, however, they became routine work to the Raiding Forces men, although the element of doubt about one's reception is always piquant at the moment. The report continues:

"We made our way up the watercourse, which we found to contain a spring, turned up Mount 'Pallucote', and eventually found an excellent hideout at approximately Map Reference...."

"The following morning the Greek officer got into touch with a shepherd, and sent him to bring up an English-speaking Greek who had helped one of the previous patrols, to a rendezvous. At 09.30 hours, the Greek officer and the war correspondent went off to the rendezvous."

The strain of lying "doggo" – as the main body had, has to be experienced to be understood. Although supposed to be resting against the coming night's work, to be behind the enemy lines, constantly in enemy territory, wondering how the Folboat party was getting on, and if the Greek lieutenant had walked into a trap, spoilt one's sleep. Yet despite it they slept.

At 17.40 hours the pair returned with their man. The report reads:

"The English-speaking islander told us that the garrison of about 50 Germans stayed in Livadia and sent daily patrols of from 3 to 10 men to Megalo Chorio. He also gave us approximate positions of the defences of Livadia area, and told us no Greeks were there. As shipping was our priority task, we decided to wait until D-plus-4 to shoot up one of the patrols and take some prisoners. The local man was to come back to us on D-plus-2 day and we would then make a recce of the road to find a suitable place for an ambush. While he was with us another shepherd, whom we called Mike, joined us; he later proved invaluable.

"Next morning, Mike arrived and offered to take one of us dressed as a Greek to a position overlooking Livadia defences. Our Greek officer went with him and was able to pinpoint gun positions and billets." (A

TERROR BY NIGHT

large-scale sketch map made as a result of this recce is attached as an appendix to the report, with these details.) "He also made a recce of the road and found an excellent position for an ambush; but it was such that we should have to attack the patrol on its way to Megalo Chorio in the morning, and not on its return... This meant that we would have any prisoners captured on our hands for at least two days, for we had to plan the attack for D-plus-4; so we asked the ship if they could pick us up on D-plus-4, which was arranged."

Communication with our H.Q. back in Egypt by portable wireless twice a day was our only link with the outside world as the M.L. had departed at speed as soon as the party was ashore in order to get under cover before dawn.

The report continues:

"On the morning of D-plus-3, Mike turned up again and said that the mayor would like to meet us; that in fact he was rather hurt that the British had not already got into touch with him. We saw no harm in meeting him and had a talk with him that afternoon. He told us that some of the Germans had got drunk in Megalo Chorio on Easter Sunday, so it had been put out of bounds for a week and no patrols would be going there except on special duty. The mayor was most co-operative, even offering to put a sleeping draught in the Germans' food or water. This was no idle offer, as he was persona grata with the Germans in Livadia and could have got into the kitchen without suspicion; and that kitchen served the whole garrison."

These raiding parties carried arms, ammunition, demolition charges, rations, medical stores and a quantity of gold sovereigns; but quantities of narcotic for putting the garrison quietly to sleep were not in the scheduled stores.

"It was decided to attempt to entice the Germans out, and the mayor agreed to see the German officer in charge, 2nd Lieut. Urbanicz, and try to persuade him to visit Megalo Chorio on D-plus-4, or D-plus-5, to attend to some business there. At 22.00 hours Mike arrived with the news that Lieut. Urbanicz was to meet the mayor in Megalo Chorio on D-plus-r.

"Corporal Hughes returned at 01.10 hours.

"Owing to the fact that Lieut. Urbanicz often visited a lady at 04.00 or 05.00 hours before attending to the business of the day, we had to leave our hideout at 02.15 hours on D-plus-4 in order to be in position in time.

"Apparently this was not one of those occasions, for it was not until 07.30 hours that Mike, who had taken up a position on the hillside, signalled to us that 4 Germans were on their way up the road.

"They came into sight 400 yards away and when they neared our position Lieut. Urbanicz, his quartermaster and personal clerk were in front, with the fourth German, a private, about 100 yards behind with a mule and a dog.

"When they were almost abreast of our ambush, we jumped out and called on them to surrender. Unfortunately they made for their guns and when it was all over the casualties were 4 Germans and 1 dog killed. The mule got off without a scratch.

"We made our way up a shallow wadi to the East, crossed over the mountain and returned to our hideout, Mike carrying the Bren. At midday the Germans fired 24 rounds from one of their guns at the upper slopes of Mount 'Cuzzoreglis', apparently mistaking some goats for us.

"That afternoon a shepherd told us that a patrol of 7 Germans had come up the road very carefully, found the bodies, returned hurriedly to Livadia and come back with seven more. These men searched the valley, and questioned the shepherds, who were very vague; they took the bodies back in a wagon. The mayor and two Greek representatives accompanied the bodies as a mark of respect."

The mayor had a difficult part to play here. Many thoughts must have been racing through his mind as he walked beside the bodies but he was never suspected.

"We were picked up from Lethra Bay at 00.15 hours by the launch."

The report finally pays tribute to the Greek officer accompanying it and records an appreciation of local inhabitants, with their occupation, location, local repute and serviceability or danger to such patrol work; and useful topographical notes, pinpointing on the map hideouts and any new information obtained.

Corporal Hughes, who went off in the Folboat with a companion four days earlier, was not able to make any attack on shipping, and returned with little gain beyond some new information; this is a normal hazard but it was not often that some material advantage could not be taken. In this case, specific instructions prevented the corporal attempting any further objectives.

His report says:

"On arrival at the landing beach, we made ready the Folboat and left the party at 01.30 hours. We expected to arrive at our destination in about an hour or an hour and a half. There was a heavy sea running, with a stern wind. Owing to poor light I did not notice that we had passed Livadia Bay, and thought that Zacharias Bay was the one containing the objective (Scala harbour)."

This bald opening is a masterly piece of understatement. The Folboat is a narrow, canoe-like craft, some 12 feet long, that folds up, and is made of rubber over a very light frame. Even a slight sea, if choppy, makes it difficult to paddle any distance and the rise and fall, plus pitching, make it difficult to pick out objects a mile off with much detail, owing to its lowness in the water, while the view is cut off each time it sinks into the trough of the waves. Keeping a lookout and paddling hard at half past one on a starlight night in such a frail shell is no easy task. They shot past their mark.

"At 02.45 hours we pulled into a sheltered creek at Map Reference.........." continues the report. "We unload the boat and emptied it of water." (The splashing waves had poured in through the openings in the canvas top and the two men had been sitting in three inches of water.)

"We spelt until 06.30 and found on waking up that we were in the wrong bay. We lay up all day, and at 23.20 hours left for Livadia Bay, arriving at 00.50 hours, 10th April. Until 02.45 we were looking for a hiding place for the Folboat.

"We lay up at Map Reference......... until 06.30 hours, and then established an O.P. at Map Reference........ but nothing of any importance was seen, as all the other objectives came under the main party's scope. No shipping was seen during our stay at the O.P.

DEATH VISITS TILOS

"We left to rejoin the main party at 00.30 hours 12th April, meeting them at the main landing beach at 01.10 hours. The Folboat was concealed in a hideout that had been found for us, and then moved on to the main hideout. The landing place at Map Reference.............. is useless."

The whole party being reassembled and the ship signalled in, all details were withdrawn under cover of darkness.[1]

[1] Tilos was revisited in March 1945 by Raiding Forces Aegean, this time with two Indian companies under command. The German garrison surrendered on the first day.

Reconnaissance on Nisyros

Some of the intrusions upon enemy-held islands made by Raiding Forces were solely for gathering information. Such a reconnaissance was made on Nisyros in July 1944, by three Greeks under command of one of their own officers, and were landed from the Anglo Hellenic Service Caique No. 6, a small blue tub that performed prodigious service in this campaign.

Rough weather delayed the landing a day, and it was impossible for them to be put ashore at the spot planned. However, they landed safely on the island, collected their information and a dozen islanders as volunteers for the Greek Sacred Regiment and returned by motor launch to their base without incident. This small island had approximately 50 Germans and between 30 and 40 Italians as garrison. How the information was collected is told in their report.

"There are two defended areas in the island map references given and there has been no change in the defence scheme for the past two months. At Cape Akrotiri the garrison consists of about 40 Germans and a few Italian camp followers. At Pali there are about 25 Italians and 10 Germans.

"The Cape Akrotiri position is covered by a double row of wire on the south and a single row on the east as far as the breakwater. On the western side, there is a single row on the shore, and it runs to the most northerly point of Akrotiri. From here to the breakwater on the other side there is no wire. The area inside the wire is mined.

"The one gun, probably a 75mm is on the most northerly point of Akrotiri. There are two anti-aircraft guns both 20mm on the left side of the road to the west of Akrotiri, which can be used for ground defence. L.M.G.s are shifted about, mostly sited on house roofs. The ammunition dump is in the cemetery on the southern side of Akrotiri and in the small monastery on the north. Billets are shown in the accompanying plan.

"The Pali position is surrounded by double wire with mines between and along the shore, apart from a single opening (shown on plan). There is a gun here too, probably 75mm, and one 20mm, ack ack gun. Ammunition is dumped close to guns. Germans live in the small house inside the wired area. Italians are billeted in a well-camouflaged hutment, inside the wire.

"Food: German supplies are poor. They have no sugar and only 15 sacks of badly mixed flour. This is to be exchanged for a better quality as soon as possible they have been told.

General food supplies are barely sufficient and mostly consist of dried beans. No thought is given to food for the local population and, according to the Germans themselves, they do not propose to do anything about this in the future.

"Morale: Morale of the enemy is fair. Some Germans believe that German will soon come to terms with USSR against England; others say that there will soon be an understanding with England and USA against Russia. Many have hopes of an early peace and under given conditions (such as meeting our forces outside the defenced area) would willingly give themselves up. I learn that two Italians have been trying to escape to Middle East, and hoped to get away with my party.

"Shipping: In Pali harbour there is a small motor boat (can transport up to 15 men). There is no craft over 8 tons in the island. On 27th June, three armed barges arrived and discharged some flour, wood fuel and water with 21 Italians. They came from Tilos, and sailed off again to Kardamaina, on Kos, where they discharged the wood fuel. On their return journey they picked up 40 Germans from Pali on 28th July, and went on to Tilos (destination probably ultimately Rhodes).

"Every day at 06.00 hours the Pali motor boat sails either to Mandraki harbour or to the island of Gyali, carrying water, or on patrol. Very rarely the whole island shore patrolled.

"Usual Movements: Reveille and change of guards are at dawn. At night, 12 men guard Akrotiri promontory. During the day, this guard seems to be anything between 8 and 20 men. Breakfast is at 05.30 hours; there is no queueing up but about 30 men assemble outside the cookhouse. Some seem to come over from Pali (about 6 to 8) at the same time. Lunch is at 11.30 hours, when there is a bigger concentration of men. A party leaves the defended area every day to collect wood for fuel, and this seems to be the only time they come out. For four Saturdays in succession, there has been a general concentration of the men on the eastern side of Akrotiri from 05.30 to 06.30 hours.

"Reprisals: Following the Special Boat Service raid on Nisyros, B. Kontoveris and N. Minas were arrested by the Germans and sent to Rhodes via Tilos. There is no evidence against Minas. At Kardamaina (Kos) following a raid during which six Germans were killed, N. Mavros and K. Hadzidmitris were arrested. It is said that Mavros was released. At the village of Nikia many houses, searched after a raid, were looted.

"Quislings: (full names given in each case) ……………, teacher at Emboreios village, keeps company with Germans; ………………., of Mandraki, keeps company with Germans; Katina ……………, widow, prostitute, keeps a coffee house at ………………; M………………, fisherman, black marketer, living at Pali; S…………, black marketer gives useful information but talks a lot; Mrs T……………, widow of an Italian.

"Main sources of information: at Pali: M. Roditis, the mayor; at Mandraki, N. Frantzis.

"General: All islanders are strongly pre-allied in feeling and steadfastly Greek. Fascists and the Germans are detested. Non-fascist Italians are tolerated and pitied. The Germans have officially declared that the Dodecanese islands belong to Greece, and will be handed over after the war.

"Kos: 150 Italians left this island on 30th June for an unknown destination and it is said that they will be replaced by Greek gendarmes" (these belonged to the so-called Security Police organised by the Germans in Greece and were regarded as Quislings).

"Tilos: 160 Germans and a few Italians form the garrison; there are 15 Germans stationed at Aghios Nikolaos and 30 Italians at Eristos. There are 50 Germans at Livadia, where there are no longer any civilians; about 30 Germans at Aghios Antonios and 20 to 30 Germans at Megalo Chorio.

"The aerodrome at Agios Antonios is nearly ready.

"No caiques or sailing craft are at Tilos; the island is patrolled by two groups of 8 to 10 Germans, one from Livadia and one from Megalo

RECONNAISSANCE ON NISYROS

Chorio. A wireless telegraph station is sited in the house close to the shore at Megalo Chorio, where Germans are also billeted.

"Two 'Fieseler Storch' planes have so far used Nisyros aerodrome to land, it is believed for transport and mail purposes."

This type of report was checked at intervals by succeeding recce patrols. The information was collated and counterchecked from different sources and brought up-to-date immediately before any raid was planned.

Each time a series of sketch maps would be prepared and a wealth of information would be available for briefing the patrol in the minutiae of the topography if a built-up area was to be entered. Details of routine troop movements and dispositions were, of course, invaluable in enabling the raiding party to fall upon the garrison from more or less out of a clear blue sky at the most inopportune moment for them and destroy their installations as well as killing and capturing as many men as possible. There was not much going on in the islands that the Raiding Forces did not know. This meant that each section of a raid dropped into place like a well-fitting piece of a jigsaw puzzle. So that after it was all over and the nervous Germans were wondering what disaster to expect next, an outsider would have imagined it was astonishingly easy, instead of being the result of a scheme planned to the second and carried out by men who had been trained never to miss an opportunity.

The Germans were not, of course, without their counter-espionage, and their patrols were sent out to recce for information, but their efforts to trap the raiders, particularly by securing a leakage of their intentions, were usually futile.

Here the nature of things helped the attacker; for his movements were always incalculable – he didn't know himself where he would strike next, because he sought targets of opportunity. He also varied his pattern in raiding as often as possible. Despite their presence in overwhelming force the Germans found their occupation of the Greek islands anything but a rest from the strain of war, and many of them were sent back suffering from nervous break-downs as a result of the continuous tension and the waiting for a disaster that inevitable happened.

Five Headaches on Paros

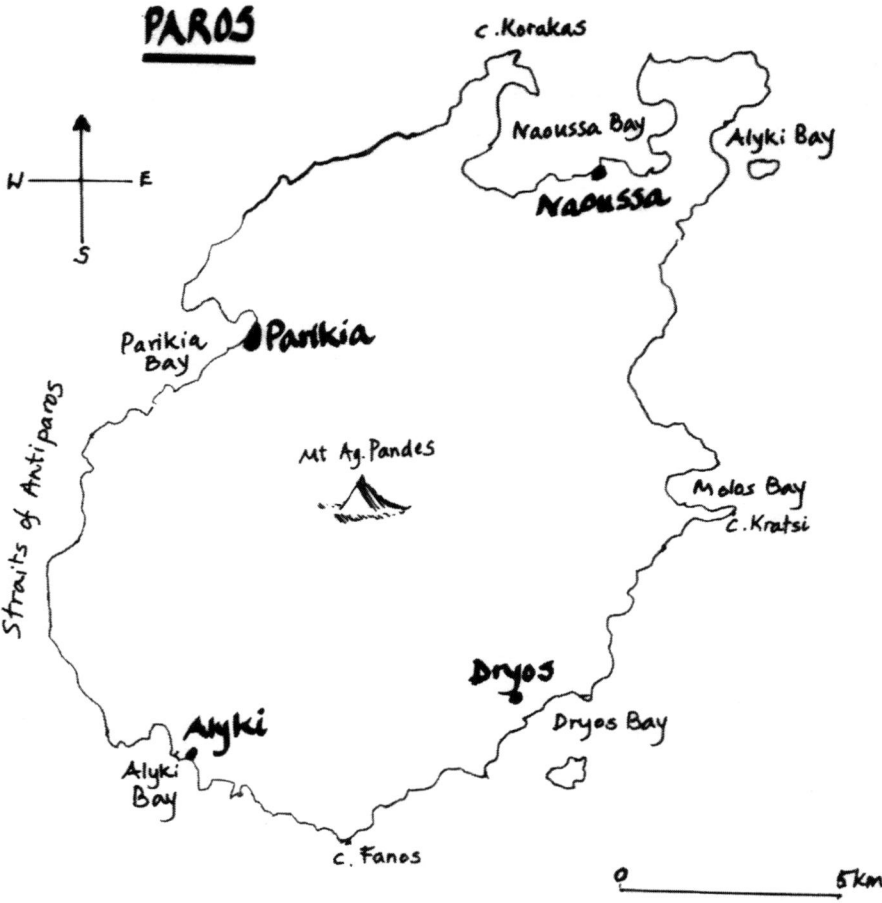

Five separate tasks were allotted to a party of 18 all ranks that went to Paros in May 1944. It was an ambitious programme that illustrates how to unforeseen always crops up. What the effect of the multiple attack must have been on the overstrained nerves and morale of the German garrison after the raiding patrol had sailed away must be left to the imagination of the reader.

Orders were to capture or destroy enemy shipping in Paros harbours, to demolish equipment and in particular to attend to an aerodrome. Finally there was a "blanket" instruction to attack enemy communications and personnel.

The sortie was to sail on 9th May, lie up during daylight on the 10th and 11th, and land the night of the 11th. The party was then to go to the house of a certain Gero Vangelis, who would provide a reliable guide, after which they would collect the necessary intelligence and signal intentions to H.Q., when ready to act.

Single-letter signals formed a code to be flashed to a small naval motor launch when the party was ready to be picked up, after the operation at one of three points on the seashore, as necessity might dictate; the ship was to be standing by on the night of 15th May and would act in accordance with the letter flashed.

The party took 6 days' rations, 3 light machine guns, 48 grenades, a dozen "76" grenades, 42 Lewis bombs, 8 kg of candles and 20 sovereigns.

The sovereigns were a regular part of raiding material; worth approximately five paper pounds. They made an invaluable persuader when coercion was too noisy, a couple of these gold pounds sometimes kept things quiet long enough for the raiders to get away. In the main though they were used to reward the many Greeks who came forward out of patriotism to help Raiding Forces, at the risk of their lives.

The raiding party, including one British and one Greek officer, wet out on the job on the day planned but then were weather-bound for four days, which put all the timings forward. They landed safely on an isolated beach, at half past one in the morning, and marched all night to the highest point on Paros called Koromboli, overlooking the aerodrome.

Dawn forced them to stay there through the day, and they started the march again at dusk and reached a hideout some hours later, where they laid-up for the day while information was being gathered. That night they made their attack.

The plan called for close co-ordination of the various attacks in order to secure the maximum effect. The individual items were as follows:

TERROR BY NIGHT

Captain "Andy" Lassen, M.C., was to take three men to attack a gun position. This plan was foiled when the alarm was given before his party were near enough to attack. The gun stood in an open field and was liberally protected with trenches. The gun crew and guard of twenty Germans stood to on the first warning from the sentry and fired Verey lights to put other posts on the alert and summon reinforcements.

Without the element of surprise, outnumbered by five to one and faced with resolute defenders prepared to fight it out, Captain Lassen and his party regretfully withdrew.

Sgt. P. Henderson, with Corporal d'Arcy and Parachutist Jarrell, on another mission, were handicapped by this premature alarm, and also by a trail of barking from the dogs of the cottages they passed. This pinpointed their position and could not be avoided.

"We left at 21.15 hours, with a Greek guide and an interpreter to deal with a wireless station in the town of Draghoulas" reads Sgt. Henderson's report. "At a point north-west of the town, the guide refused to go any further and seemed highly nervous.

"He gave us an intricate description of how to reach the target, which was quite different from our previous information, so we sent him and the interpreter back to Capt. Lassen to report that we were going into the town to try and locate the post by asking at houses we passed."

The three men crept along in shelter of a stone wall, towards where they imagined their objective to be, when suddenly they heard firing and saw the alarm signals given when Captain Lassen's party was discovered. The time was about half past ten, Sgt. Henderson made his way right round the edge of the town and entered again from the opposite direction; but as the alarm had sounded, none of the Greeks they tried to knock up would come to their doors.

This baffled them as far as their own objective went, so Sgt. Henderson decided to join one of the other parties and help them. He went towards Marpissa, where another wireless station was to receive attention but when he got near, a confusion of shots and explosions broke out. Obviously, it was too late to join that party; and again the dogs started barking.

FIVE HEADACHES ON PAROS

"We were forced to make another large circle to avoid leaving a trail of barking dogs to the pick-up point," adds Sgt. Henderson.

He got his party to the beach south of the rendezvous, but the ship was invisible; and he could not flash his torch for fear of endangering the motor launch. So he found a hiding place and kept his party hidden till the following night, and remarks prosaically that "we contacted the H.D.M.L. at the alternative pick-up point" the following evening, by which time the other parties were all aboard".

In view of the enemy "flap" on the island, Sgt. Henderson's party was greeted with some relief when they came on board as even in the best planned ops there is the chance of an accident.

Parachutist Perkins accompanied an officer and a corporal of the Greek Sacred Regiment to attack a wireless station "and personnel" in the town of Marpissa.

"I was detailed to go forward and make a recce," he reports. "The approach was easy, and after watching closely I saw there was a German officer with three men in the house. But when I returned, they must have heard me; for as we were going up the steps of the house, we were met by the German officer standing at the far end of the verandah. He was silhouetted in a doorway, with a pistol in his hand. We had orders to take prisoners if possible so I said to him in German, "Hands up! It's all over". He replied, "What" and fired a shot. I returned his fire and hit him in the stomach. The Greek corporal shot him too, with a tommy-gun, and he died in a few seconds.

"Then we threw a grenade into the wireless room through the window, and another grenade into another room. I think the first one put the wireless out of action. The Greek officer shot the French windows on the verandah open and we went in.

"There the Greek officer and I killed one each and the corporal wounded the third. The injured man continued firing at us, however, and the Greek officer shot him again and finished him off.

"After that we made our way through the town, towards the rendezvous; but as a small piece of shrapnel from the second grenade had entered my right leg, and the Greek officer had some pieces in his right arm and chest, our progress was slow."

They reached the ship all right, however, and Parachutist Perkins adds that the radio was left unfit for use, although the engine to produce the power was still in working order.

Cpl. J. Sibbet, Parachutist Hancock and a Greek guide set off to blow up a bomb and petrol dump and got very near it; in fact, they passed the first two German posts and then fifty yards from the target when they felt they were well down the home stretch they tripped over some camouflage among the rocks. As it was an extremely dark night they made investigations as cautiously as they could, but the slight noises disturbed a sentry who came out of a post among the rocks and fired at them.

"We made off for a short distance, hoping to be taken for local Greeks," reported Cpl. Sibbet; "but the guard was burned out, and Verey lights were fired in our direction while machine guns opened up on us with tracer bullets and we had to abandon the objective."

They made their way back to the beach, trying to avoid villages and their own patrols as well as any enemy patrols.

"Our guide was very excitable", he adds. "He pointed out our objective all right, but while we were examining the camouflage, he vanished. The sentry post was not mentioned in the information we had previously received."

Sgt. J. Nicholson, M.M., who had earned a repute for making a workmanlike job of his tasks, submits a brief report of a very effective little operation. Accompanied by Lance Corporal Bartie and Marine Williams, his job was to tackle a house were a German officer lived with two German soldiers.

The attack was to be launched at a quarter to midnight, but before his party was quite in position a large explosion in the town blew the gaff. So Sgt. Nicholson told his lance corporal to toss a hand grenade through the upstairs window while he and the marine forced their entry.

"We each took a separate room, while L/Cpl. Bartie remained outside

FIVE HEADACHES ON PAROS

on watch as I had heard people running about in the town," he says. "On entering the room, I found it empty; so I went into another. The German officer was hiding behind a door. I made him prisoner."

Marine Williams found one man, killed by the grenade they had thrown, in his room, and there was nobody else in the house.

On their way back to the rendezvous a patrol spotted this party and opened fire, and the German officer was wounded in the neck. Knowing that the enemy was confused by the noise and darkness and could have no accurate idea of the true state of affairs despite the hue and cry, Sgt. Nicholson carried on towards the rendezvous, merely pausing to put first aid dressing on the German's wound.

"Further on", he said, "another patrol threw two grenades at us, and the German officer was hit again. We left him for dead and returned to the rendezvous."

In his report, the commander of the party observed that the islanders themselves in Paros had not been helpful; the airfield was well defended, and three additional companies were expected shortly to strengthen the defence.

On the first alarm being sounded, all German troops stood-to except the base personnel in the town. He adds of these "chairborne" troops that there were only 12 of them, that they took no precautions, leaving the defence to the others, and that eight of them became casualties.

This brief account of the raid exemplifies the principle of hit and run, in action with the careful avoidance of engagements when the raiding party was up against an alert enemy of superior numbers.

When the element of surprise was absent, the raiders dropped their plan and either vanished or switched to help another party. With a multiple plan, any unforeseen snag was liable to arouse the whole garrison, and render the other objectives more difficult, but the results were satisfactory from the material standpoint. It was unlucky, in spite of St. Henderson's care of his prisoner, that none of the enemy could be brought off for interrogations; but that is one of the big hazards when withdrawing a patrol in the face of an alert and determined enemy.

One result of the raid was to heighten the Germans' sense of insecurity,

TERROR BY NIGHT

for although all the planned targets had not been dealt with according to plan, the Germans did not know the original scheme.

All that they could picture clearly were the items that had been done successfully and this undermined their morale.

They saw that even to have brave and well-disciplined troops on the alert who took post promptly and effectively on the first alarm, was not enough to guard against the "terror by night".

Part of the particular value of operations of this nature was the way in which they heartened the islanders and sustained their faith in Britain, they old ally, who they could see, was defeating the hated enemy. Later, the Germans were to find, in spite of Goebbels' reiterated propaganda, the conviction among the Greek population that the Allies were going to win. Many islands had a concealed wireless received on which the daily news in Greek broadcast by the B.B.C. was received.

Caiques and Cables

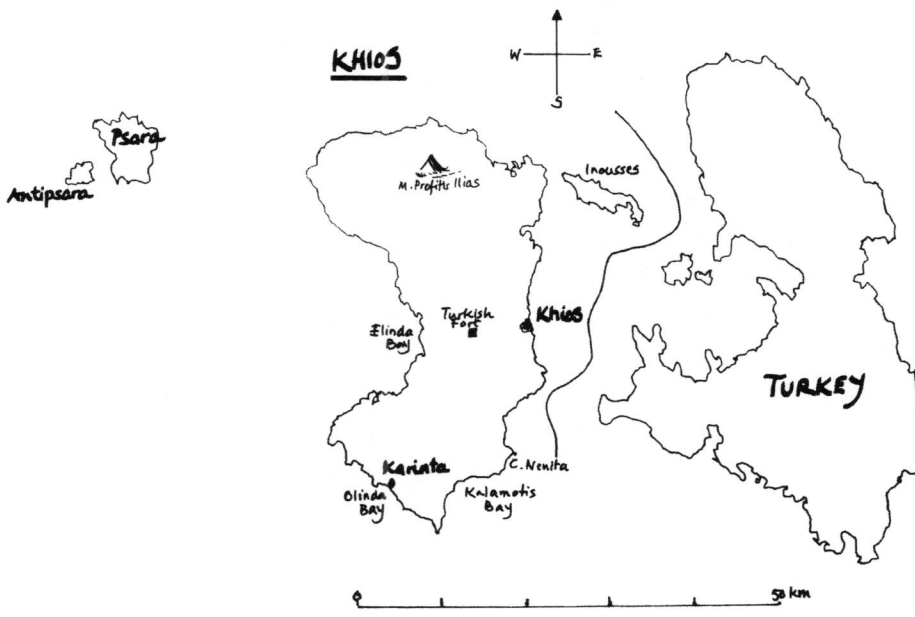

The attack on the Khios caique building and repair yards and the cable installations in June, 1944, was an excellent example of the Raiding Forces' policy of "maximum damage – minimum loss".

A mixed party of 40 British and Greek troops, under Lt-Col (now Colonel) Andreas Kolinski of the Greek Sacred Regiment left for Khios in two small H.D.M.L.s from a forward base.

Travelling by night and lying up under camouflage nets in isolated hideouts by day, the two M.L.s made the long trip without incident. Since the little ships had to pass very close to the shores of Kos and Samos it was expected the Nazis' radar would pick them up.

All hands stood to in case of an attack by E-boats and the raiders' Bren guns were mounted in addition to the M.L.'s own armament.

After three nights' travelling the vessels reached the selected landing

TERROR BY NIGHT

beach at Karinta Bay[1] in South West Khios at 01.30 hours. A line was run ashore by dinghy and the troops and supplies were disembarked in rubber boats, all getting ashore in less than half an hour.

Guides with nine mules were to meet the party on the beach and carry the mortars, mortar bombs, explosions, radio batteries and spare food, but they failed to turn up. This failing was common among the Andartes and little reliance could ever be put in their promises.

After waiting an hour for the guides, a reconnaissance was made to pick a spot where the party could lie up under cover for the day. As there was a possibility of the Nazis having intercepted the guides and mules a good defensive location had to be chosen as well as having plenty of cover.

Guards were posted and the rest of the party settled down for a good sleep in the olive grove and under the shadow of the dry-stone walls. Few of them had had more than naps since the expedition started, owing to the overcrowding on the M.L.s and the fact they could not go ashore by day.

At dusk the mule loads were divided among the raiders and what it was not possible for them to add to their already heavy packs was buried. Just then two men with mules arrived and said the others would not come. They did not seem in the least abashed to be a day late.

The two mules just managed to carry the supplies that had been buried and the party set off up a winding trail which led to the top of the mountains overlooking the landing beach.

Two hours and 1500 feet later, the party took a last look at the sea and turned inland across a plateau surfaced with small rough stones and broken with scrub bushes.

Although carrying very heavy packs the raiders marched hard. They had to cover 22 miles in 7 hours, only an average of just over 3 miles an hour but most of it was up and down hillsides, climbing rather than marching up steep, dry watercourses and hurrying along goat tracks.

The objective of the night's march was an old Turkish fortified camp in

---

1 Possibly Elinda Bay due West of Khios.

CAIQUES AND CABLES

the middle of pinewoods, some 15 miles from Khios town, but high up in the mountains.

It was just first light as the last men trudged into the camp. One of the delays in the night had occurred when the mule with the reserve food on it, slipped and rolled down a hillside, scattering its burden, which could not be recovered.

With the exception of sentries and a M.G. post crew, everyone slept until lunch time when some of the G.S.R.[ii] put on civilian clothes and went down to contact our agents in the town and surrounding villages. At last all the information was collected but still things occurred to delay the attack.

The final delay was due to the main item of the operation, the "mopping up" of the garrison of 184 men. It had been planned that the R.A.F. would drop seven and a half tons of bombs, mixed high explosive and incendiary, in the garrison perimeter. During the time when the garrison was under cover, two parties would deal with the caique yards and cables and then unite with the main party which was watching to prevent any breakout from the perimeter.

The reunited force would then go through gaps in the enemy's wire and clean up the survivors.

At the last moment, the R.A.F. radioed that their part of the operation over the perimeter was off. In their examination of an air photograph they had noticed a building with Red Crosses on it in the middle of the target area.

On liberation, it was found to be the main garrison petrol store.

Meanwhile a recce patrol made a final survey of the town through field glasses. From a neighbouring hill every detail stood out sharply in the clear sunshine – each individual caique in the boatyard – one of the main objectives.

A few hours before attacking, the party were assembled for a final briefing. The force was divided into four patrols, the first to attack the caique yards

2 During April 1944, the Greek Sacred Squadron was upgraded to Regimental status.

and destroy all the vessels; the second to destroy the cables and the cable station; the third to act as a covering party for the withdrawal, and the last one to liquidate two German posts on the line of retreat.

Then followed a 15-mile march into the town – to be followed by several more miles to the point where the party must be picked up. For the first part of the way the force marched together, down steep tracks and stony watercourses.

At the first halt they broke up – each party going off in a different direction. On the outskirts of one tiny village a man was seen. He was riding a donkey, and keeping a course diagonal to that of the armed intruders. He carefully avoided looking at them, the whole time they were in sight.

As one party went through a village, all the men and women, who were gardening, ostentatiously kept their backs turned. It recalled the line in Kipling's smuggling song – "Watch the wall, my darling, while the gentlemen go by...".

If any of those islanders had been questioned by the Germans after the raid, they could honestly say they had not seen the raiding force.

The first party headed for the caiques which lay in the Northern sector of the harbour, while the main German defence area protected by mines and barbed wire was on the Southeast side, only 400 yards across the water.

Treading as softly as they could, the party entered the town from the Northwest, and marching in open order through the deserted streets, gained the outskirts of the old fortress and followed round the walls.

Expecting every moment to be challenged by a German patrol, they reached the East Gate without being seen and got through. This was the last lap. At the end of the street was the caique yard, with thirteen caiques drawn up at the quay. A Bren gun was set up as protection against a possible German attack from their main position across the harbour.

Suddenly the civilians moved aside and revealed a small group of German soldiers. But it was impossible for the moment to fire on the Germans without hitting the islanders.

Then some sound must have reached the enemy group, for the Germans turned and came towards our party, who were now able to open fire with sub-machine guns. Two of the Germans fell dead, and three others were wounded. Strangely enough, not one shot came from the main enemy post, and it seemed likely that a strong patrol was being sent out to tackle the invaders.

It was imperative to finish the business of destroying the caiques without any delay.

While some of the party placed the charges, the remainder watched for an attack. The attack failed to materialise, and when all the charges had been successfully laid, the party withdrew to watch the explosions.

These came in quick succession. The whole of the thirteen caiques went up – eleven coasting vessels and two larger armed ones which had been used for escort purposes on inter-island trips. They had suddenly become a rain of broken timber falling into the harbour and on to the quay.

This did at last rouse the German garrison. But all they did in reply was to send a few bursts off ill-aimed machine gun fire which did no harm to the party.

During the withdrawal, further explosions shook the ground – the cable-house had been dealt with, and the cables had gone too. In fact, all four parties had had a highly successful trip. Two of them had found their objectives ungarrisoned.

Without a casualty Raiding Forces had caused the Germans thousands of pounds worth of damage, and launched another severe blow at their morale.

Marooned on Kos

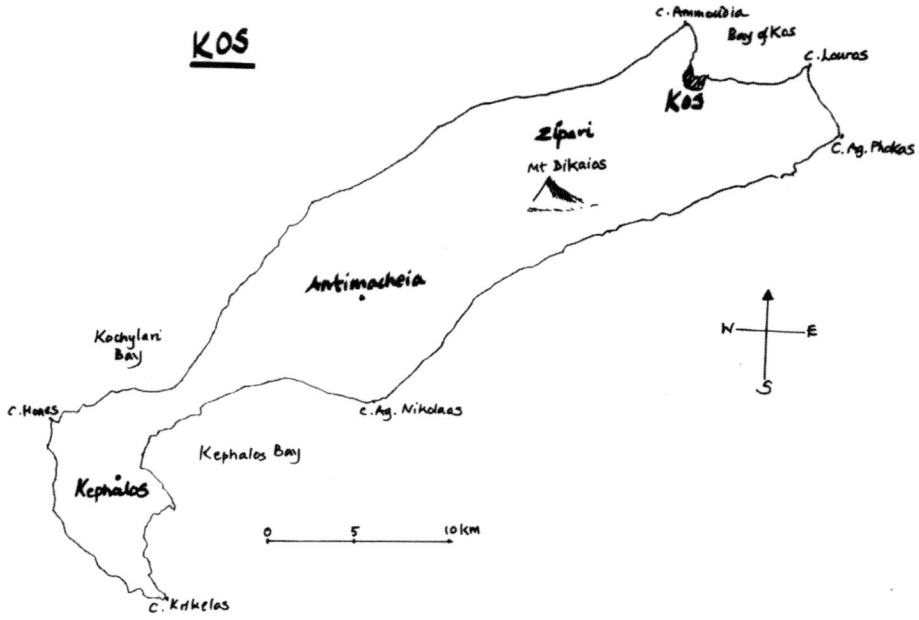

After being marooned on Kos, during the German occupation, with their radio set out of order and with scanty rations, a Raiding Force patrol carried out the reconnaissances they had been detailed to perform and were safely evacuated by the Royal Navy.

Trouble dogged the patrol right from the start, perhaps because they started 13 men strong at 13.00 hours on the 13th of the month.

Coming in to land on the coast of the island not far from Antimacheia, the patrol was just about to lower the collapsible boat to cover the last couple of hundred yards to the shore when they were fired on by machine guns, sub-machine guns and mortars.

With coloured Verey lights illuminating the sky the naval vessel put about quickly to get away from the dangerous coastline. It was then decided that a second attempt would be made to put the patrol ashore at a different spot two days later.

MAROONED ON KOS

The landing ship lay just over a mile from the short of Kos, when the collapsible rubber boat and a small dinghy were launched into the oily swell. In the dinghy were an officer and a signalman. They had with them the radio set and a battery, the other battery being carried by the patrol's second signalman.

"When we had got all the gear into the boat", said the signalman, "it was pretty full and there was only about an inch of freeboard, but as we had been told we were only a couple of hundred yards from the shore we did not worry.

"The officer was rowing and I was keeping an eye on the rubber boat that was going in ahead of us. It was soon quite clear that we were a long way further than 200 yards from the shore and to make matters worse the wind was getting up and the oil swell was splashing water into our tiny boat.

"She got more and more difficult to handle and we lost sight of the rubber boat; eventually the boat became waterlogged and would have sunk if the two of us had not got out and swum, supported by our "Mae Wests" and pushing the boat. After some hours we managed to get ashore in a somewhat exhausted condition.

"Although the boat was waterlogged, the batteries were undamaged having been carefully waterproofed before we left. After emptying the boat, the officer and I set out in opposite directions to try and find the rest of the patrol, but could not find them.

"We then got into the boat again, having buried the batteries, with the intention of going back towards the naval vessel and thus getting a line on where the rest of the patrol were landing. But by this time the wind and sea had got up considerably and we were swamped before we could get 20 yards away from the shore.

"Each time we got swamped we emptied the boat and tried again, but having tried solidly from midnight until three in the morning we were exhausted and had to give up. We sank the dinghy with large rocks and then moved off to find somewhere to hide for the day.

"Wet through and tired out, after swimming round several cliff promontories we at last found the mouth of a wadi and found cover in a bush on a hillside. Our supplies consisted of two tins of self-heating soup, two tins of bully and some tea milk and sugar in a tin. Everything else had been ruined by immersion in the sea water.

"We slept until noon, our wet clothes drying on us, and then shared a tin of soup. Dozing in turn through the afternoon we made a tiny brew of tea about six o'clock and then waited for dark. About half past nine it was safe to leave our hideout, and in about half an hour we met the rest of the patrol coming our way.

The other members of the party had had an equally adventurous time. The rubber boat had developed a leak, with the result that it had partly deflated and everything was soaked. This, plus the wind and tide, had delayed the landing and it was almost dawn when the last men were ashore, so they had hidden for the day, in a cave on the shore about two miles from us.

After establishing headquarters in a series of caves in a dry wadi the patrol found that the wireless set was useless as a result of its immersion in the sea and that to last 14 men for seven days they had four small packs of biscuits, 25 tins of soup, 20 tins of bully, a little sea-soaked oatmeal and some tea sugar and milk.

Strict rationing was introduced by the officer commanding and the day's dietary consisted of: - Breakfast: a quarter pint of thin salt porridge, Lunch: half a pint of tea and a biscuit, Supper: five spoonfuls of thin bully stew and a couple of biscuits.

"It was a pretty lean time for all of us," one of the patrol said, "we had to keep the tins of soup in case anyone got wounded, but on the third day we contacted a shepherd who agreed to bring us what food he could get that day. This consisted of cucumbers, a few figs and fewer eggs.

"However, with this we were able to increase the lunch ration by one boiled egg, two figs and a cucumber. I don't think I have ever been quite so hungry in my life as while this was going on we were making reconnaissances to see what was happening on Antimacheia aerodrome and at Kos town itself."

"To do this, we had to do long arduous marches in the pitch dark, up rugged mountains, crawling along narrow ridges where a slip would have meant serious injury, if not death. It was alright at first but as we got hungrier and hungrier it became more of an effort and towards the end it was a hard day's work just get up to our observation eyrie.

"One morning we saw six big lighters full of stores come into Kos harbour and would have given a lot for a working radio set so that we could have put the R.A.F. onto the target."

Another party was keeping an eye on the aerodrome and it was a real punishing trip for them to get up to the spot where they watched from. In addition, they were too tired to carry much gear and so nearly froze on the top of the mountain at about three in the morning.

Another of the troubles that affected the patrol as a whole was that all the available water was tainted with sulphur and did not quench the thirst.

On the day the patrol left the island the shepherd lad who had been bringing the cucumbers also produced a small kid which gave everyone new heart, although there was not very much each as by this time the party had been increased by four.

These were the shepherd lad and his cousin and two girls. One of them aged 16 was the fiancée of the elder shepherd. The Germans were planning, as she was an orphan, to put into the military brothel in Kos town. The other girl aged 14 was motherless and had been living with the elder one.

At last came the time to leave the island. Slowly and noiselessly the patrol and four refugees made their way to a hiding place on the seashore and flashed the recognition signal to the waiting naval vessel, a moment's pause and then the agreed reply.

Sentries with machine guns were posted to guard the approaches to the beach as the vessel nosed into the shore, small boats came off and in less than half an hour everyone was safely on board. Another recce patrol had done its job and returned safely to base.

Party on Symi

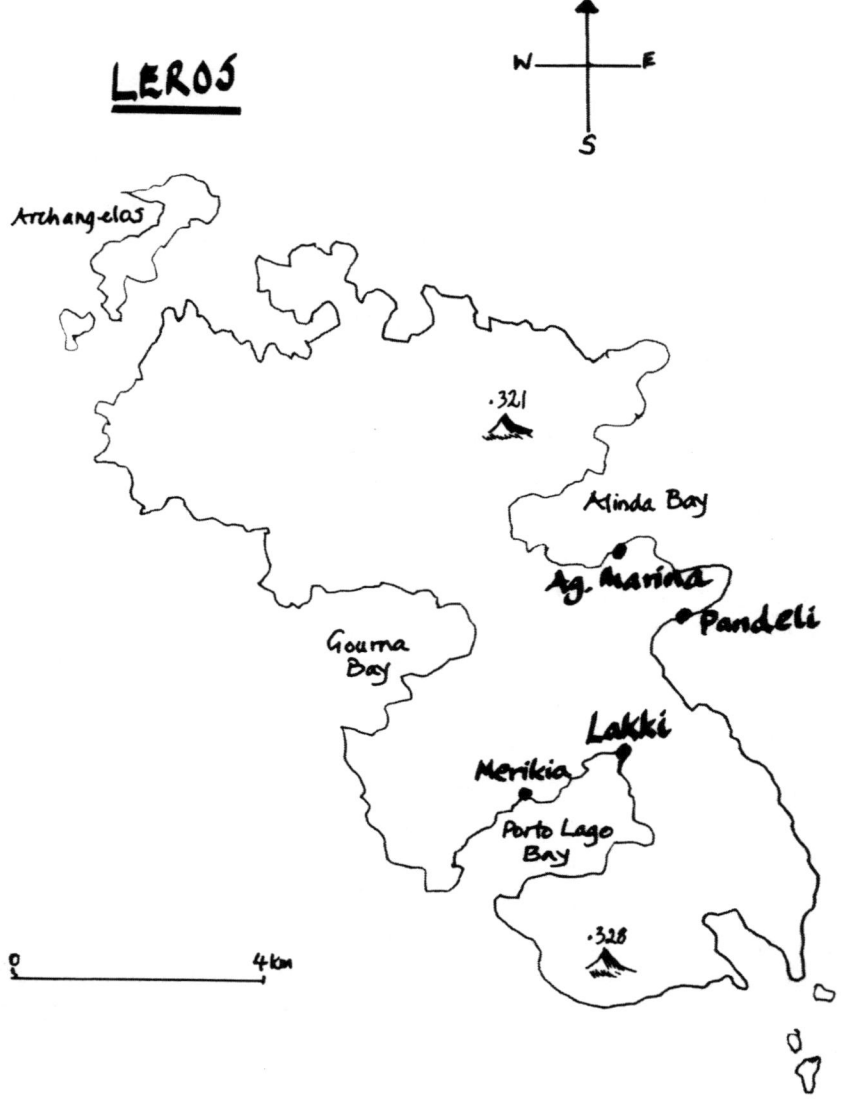

On July 14th came the Symi operation – prototype of the raids which followed the establishment of Khios as H.Q. and for this reason personally led by the commander and his G1 Lt-Col Lapraik.

PARTY ON SYMI

This operation had been considered for some time, but because the enemy had four destroyers in the Aegean it did not look practicable. Then, when two of these were sunk, the prospects materially improved. It was decided that a raiding force could take care of the other two destroyers and thus leave the sea free for the operation on Simi.

"A party of the Royal Marine Boom Control detachment put off in their folding canoes from an M.L. a mile off Porto Lago entrance to Lakki on the island of Leros," said Q.M.S. Alexander Fraser, R.A.C., parachutist-chief clerk of Raiding Forces, recalling the adventure. "The canoes were paddled into the harbour where the German destroyers lay, and planted charges against their sides. When the canoes left the harbour, they left pandemonium behind them. Explosions, flares, Verey lights, guns – everything was going off."

The main stumbling block to Operation "Tenement", as the Symi raid was called, had been removed.

But there were other difficulties. Our force had to be concentrated near enough to the objective for the return journey to be made during the hours of darkness. And troops had to be collected from such widely dispersed areas as Palestine, Alexandria, and Cairo, while a large part of the force was already operation widely dispersed over the Aegean. This difficulty was overcome by concentrating in stages – the caiques and M.L.s anchoring in coves and inlets, and remaining there, camouflaged, some of them for weeks.

After detailed recces, the plan was made. It was decided to attack in daylight because the enemy was now "standing to" during the night, and "standing down" by day.

Powered dories sped to and fro the bays and inlets where our caiques and M.L.s lay, carrying the orders for the co-ordination of the attack. It was the only way in which the necessarily scattered detachments could be briefed.

By 22.30 hours on 13th July the concentration of our forces was effected. They comprised 224 officers and men in three parties.

The main force with M.M.G.s and mortars completed their landing at Agia Marina beach at 01.50 hours, 14th July. But it was not accomplished

without misadventure. Two of the Greek officers, heavily weighted in full equipment and with the large packs, fell out of their rubber boat. A desperate rescue effort failed, and they were drowned. It was a hard loss at the very commencement of the venture.

The West and South Force disembarked at their appointed spots without incident. But all the approach marches were over rough country strewn with boulders, and entirely without paths. Nevertheless, by 05.00 hours the three parties were in position.

As daylight broke, the hidden invaders were able to see exactly how much their task would entail. Movement was seen on the Castle ramparts – one of the objectives. Two E.M.S. craft were seen to leave the harbour – and it appeared as though these prospective victims had been lost to us. An enemy post at Molo "stood down", and gave away its positions and gaps in the wire to our patrol lying up in a Monastery 150 yards away.

The assault was now begun by a mortar and M.G. barrage on Symi Castle. It was the signal for simultaneous attacks by all parties.

Almost at the same time the two E.M.S. barges re-entered the harbour, and were enthusiastically greeted by five of our M.L.s who successfully engaged them with all guns. The E.M.S. craft entered Symi harbour and were captured by boarding by our troops.

Molo Point was captured, and one patrol advanced to within 300 yards of the Castle. Force H.Q., a Vickers M.G. and a mortar troop joined in the attack. But it had now become a three hour journey to get ammunition from the Marina Beach, and all approaches to our positions were covered at this stage by machine-guns from the Castle.

It looked like stalemate, and the force commander decided to try and bluff the enemy into surrender.

A German Petty Officer, captured from one of the E.M.S. barges, was sent under escort to the Castle with a message informing the Germans that the entire island was now in our hands and further resistance was hopeless. The Germans agreed to parley, and at 15.00 hours they surrendered.

"They came down the rocks with white flags and their hands up," said Q.M.S. Fraser. "We marched them from the Castle into the town. And while this was going on six German planes came over and began dropping bombs. But they were ten minutes too late. The trick was ours."

TERROR BY NIGHT

West Force had reduced its target, destroying all enemy ammunition and defences. The enemy garrison in Panormitis Monastery had surrendered to South Force, who cut an important cable [to Symi] there, destroyed the telephone exchange, and all enemy weapons, taking twenty-eight prisoners.

That night the force re-embarked and evacuated the island. Prisoners under escort were put in the two captured E.M.S. barges, which were manned with their own German engineers.

A party was left on the island to continue demolitions, and food – which had been sailed over in two caiques – was distributed to the hungry islanders. The enemy spent the next day bombarding the island from the air, but the remaining patrol was successfully withdrawn in the evening.

We had lost the two Greek officers who were drowned, and six other British and Greek personnel were wounded. We destroyed two ammunition and explosive dumps, guns, a W/T station, 'phone exchange, a fuel dump, fortifications, nineteen caiques – amounting to 970 tons – in various stages of construction, and captured the two E.M.S. barges, which were still in serviceable condition.

The operation had been a complete success and fulfilled all intentions.

PART III

Bigger and Better Raids

The second phase of Raiding Forces' work in the Aegean opened with the establishment of a permanent headquarters on the island of Khios on 28th September 1944. Through an oversight, this news was announced prematurely by the BBC, giving information of enormous value to the Germans. It showed them the focal point to be watched for early information of Raiding Force intentions and one from which the departure of patrols was hard to hide.

The Germans soon found out that their scrap of information was of trifling value, for the raids of Phase Two were even more calculated to cause alarm and despondency among the enemy than those of Phase One.

The new policy was to wipe out the entire garrison of an island and then add the island to the list of those already liberated by Raiding Forces. There was only one proviso – the odds must not be too long, that is, no garrison to be more than six times the size of the attacking force. This was an abrupt divergence from the initial scheme of harassing the Hun. Where in the old days patrols had been content to mop up an isolated post and disappear, they now eliminated entire enemy garrisons and remained.

The experimental operation to try out the newly evolved technique had taken place nearly three months before against Symi, where a largescale raid, commanded by Brigadier Turnbull, had wiped out the entire garrison at trivial cost to Raiding Forces. This attack was to become the text book operation for Phase Two. Perfectly planned and almost as well executed, it showed, as clearly as it was successful, the limits beyond which Raiding Forces could not pass.

All the islands, barring the hard core of the Aegean operation of 1943, were ripe for the plucking, but Kos, Leros, Rhodes and certain satellites were unsuitable for the new technique. On them the old type harassing raids would have to be continued.

Church bells rang and the entire population turned out to welcome the British and Greek liberators when they arrived on Khios. Men and women flocked around the troops and shook and kissed their hands, chaired them, and generally mafficked.

It was an affecting sight. Here was a people who had been under harsh enemy rule for nearly four years, if not actually starving they had been so short of food as to show the marks of malnutrition, while during the occupation they had seen industry and commerce dwindle and die, while the currency had been so inflated by the Germans as to be valueless – a five-million drachma note lay in the gutter, even the passing children disregarded it as a possible toy. Yet that worthless scrap of paper would have been worth some £39,000 before the war.

Systematic looting and requisitioning by the Germans had deprived the islanders not only of the comforts of life but of its very necessities. Yet, when the British and Greek troops arrived they were eager to show their hospitality to the British troops, and were deeply hurt if, because of their poverty, a glass of wine or a meal were refused.

And the friendliness persisted.

When an island is liberated from enemy rule hunger does not vanish, and give place to plenty, the same day; not even, at times, within a month can more be done (when the war goes on elsewhere) than to bring enough food to keep the population from further malnutrition and to bring urgent and essential medicines for the sick. So Khios was not immediately changed from a hunger-haunted prison into a land of plenty, flags and brass bands notwithstanding.

Yet the people were patient, despite empty stomachs, and continued to waylay the soldier and welcome him with smiles and expressions of gratitude that usually left him very embarrassed, and to invite him into their houses to take a glass of wine and eat a few figs or mandarins. The children never ceased to regard the British as Heroes!

Language acted as no barrier to friendships between the Greek population and the British troops, although modern Greek is one of the harder European tongues for an Englishman to learn. The sincerity of this friendship was proved by the way it stood up to the misfortunes

BIGGER AND BETTER RAIDS

that followed liberation. It survived the fact that his arrival had not brought perpetual Christmas to these people, as their welcome might have led him to believe they had expected, and the fact that the caique-loads of food, which had been hoped for, took a long while to come. The little, however, that did come was not merely welcome, it was vital to the survival of the islanders.

One of the first islands to be liberated in this phase was Samos, the scene a year before of the gallant but ill-fated effort of the Aegean Force to wrest control of the islands from the Germans when Italy collapsed. The Greek Sacred Regiment had leaped from the skies to liberate the island, on their first operational jump, only to be compelled to withdraw a few days later in the face of the German's enormous superiority in men and material.[i]

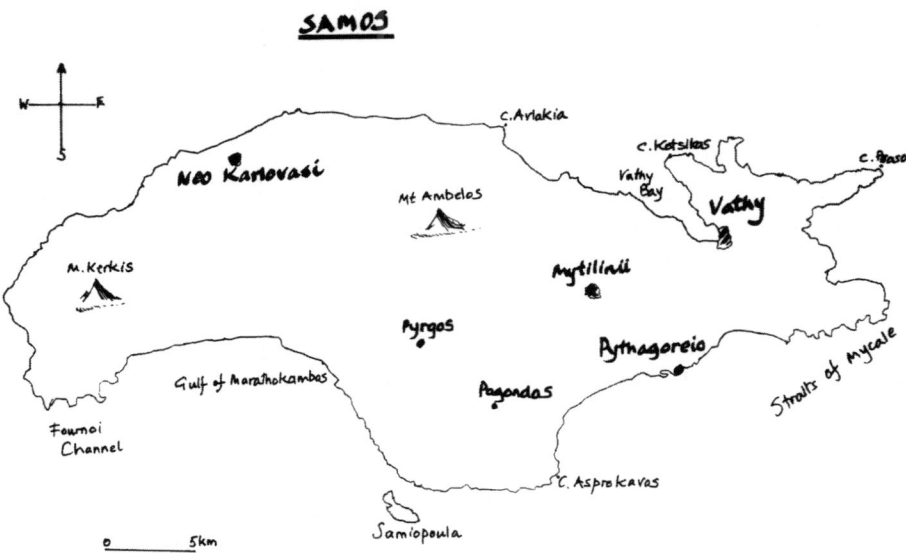

At the time of the liberation the Samos garrison consisted of about 1200 Fascist Italians, so, no doubt, bearing in mind his odds of six to one in favour of the enemy, the Commander Raiding Forces sent two motor

---

[i] Samos had also been raided by The Greek Sacred Squadron on 17 May 1944 when they attacked the garrison at Marathekampos.

launches from Khios at 08.00 hours on the morning of 3rd October 1944, with twenty-four Greek Sacred Regiment troops under the command of Colonel T. Tsigantis. In a rough sea the ships rolled heavily till 01.00 hours next morning, when they hove to and tied up to the long stone mole enclosing one side of the harbour of Karlovasi.

Although it was a brilliant moonlight night the mole was a pool of darkness, hiding in the dense shadow thrown by the hills of Samos which rise steeply behind the town. The small party of Greek soldiers made their way to the wharf and harbour town, Karlovassi is divided into three distinct townlets, and spread out, with their sub-machine guns ready if the Italian garrison wanted to fight it out. Like ghosts, in their rubber soled parachuting boots, they slid silently from shadow to shadow among the oak trees that line the main street.

Nothing moved and a feeling of serenity spread through the force; for it was anticipated that the intensive underground work of an English secret agent on the island during the previous two months would bring about the surrender of the entire Italian garrison without a shot being fired.

After they had been ashore some twenty minutes, a faint rumble broke the silence, to be replaced by the rattling sound of old cans as it got closer. It was an incredibly decrepit lorry bringing a load of Andartes to the wharf.

They reported to Colonel Tsigantes that some garrisons of the island villages were ready to surrender, and that in a couple of other garrison centres the commandants were wavering.

This report turned out to be correct. But it was always possible the Andartes had not sized the situation up accurately, or had been led up the garden path by some of the Italians; so the next business was to confirm things.

Vathy, the capital, refused all thoughts of surrender, and most of the Italian garrisons awaited the outcome of this before making a decision. A very interesting period ensued; Karlovasi had woken up to find that the forces of liberation had landed at its wharf and promptly celebrated. Church bells rang and the people rejoiced but shortage of food and the uncertainty of when supplies would be landed prevented any wild merriment. But still one thing was certain, this was the liberation, and it was final. The Greek troops had gone on, under Colonel Tsigantes' orders, right across the island to Vathy, leaving behind only two or three British officers, but they were feted as representatives of Britain to give point to the celebrations. Karlovasi had, after all, an intimate knowledge of the temper of affairs; a number of its people had done valuable under-cover work for the allies during the enemy occupation, they were in touch with the Andartes and knew what Italian and German troops had deserted to them. The information they gave was correct.

There was also a British officer on a secret service mission on the island, who had been there for some weeks, keeping touch with the Andartes and disaffected members of the enemy garrisons; but he was away at the moment in another part of Samos consolidating the final approach moves in what it was hoped would be a bloodless victory.

The state to which the island had been reduced during the occupation is made clear by the fact that when the Military Liaison Officer wanted to contact one of the Greek officers to form a Committee of local citizens for the distribution of food supplies, which he hoped would arrive at any time in a caique, he had to use a runner as there was no other form of intercommunication between the various towns and villages of the island.

When Brigadier Turnbull arrived on the island the situation at Vathy was a stalemate. The Italians were more than a match, with their heavy weapons and strongly fortified positions for the score of Greek soldiers, but they were told by the Raiders, that it was only a matter of a few days at most before overwhelming reinforcements would be brought in, if they insisted on fighting. In actual fact no reinforcements at all were available except the small party with the Brigadier and they already had jobs assigned them.

Despite these negotiations carried on by Colonel Tsigantes, and the warning of vast reinforcements available, the main garrison of the capital refused to surrender.

Brigadier Turnbull decided that further bluff was the only way to avoid a sharp engagement, which would reveal the fact that Colonel

TERROR BY NIGHT

Tsigantes had only a score of men with him. A radio signal was sent to the Italian Commandant saying that Brigadier Turnbull was advancing on Vathy with reinforcements and that if the Italians did not surrender immediately he would call on the Navy and R.A.F. to obliterate the Italians' stronghold.

The bluff worked and the Italian commandant had agreed to surrender his force to Colonel Tsigantes before Brigadier Turnbull reached Vathy. At no time did the Italians realise that the force calling on them to surrender was only a score of men, nor did they know, until too late, that Brigadier Turnbull's reinforcements consisted of only another 24 men.

Twelve hundred Italians in well-fortified strongpoints with artillery and every munition of war to carry on the struggle, gave in to 50 soldiers carrying small arms and light machine guns and whose only real offensive weapon was a 3" mortar.

Next day, the news reached Karlovasi that the remaining Italian garrison had surrendered, and the rejoicing went from village to village as the news spread. Meantime, parties of Greek soldiers were visiting the outlying Italian posts with an Italian officer, disarming them and arranging for their concentration in a prisoner of war cage. This was done without any fireworks, although some of the outlying garrisons were in fear of their lives from the Andartes, who, they expected, would cut their throats as soon as they were known to be disarmed.

To allay their fears, and because there were not enough Greek troops to form guards for every party, the old situation arose of surrendered prisoners being allowed to retain, perhaps three rifles to a dozen men, until they reached the prisoner of war cage.

Colonel Tsigantis had met the Italian commandant and also Kosta Zafiris, head of the local Andartes, and plans for the official handing over the island were going forward smoothly. There was some delay before they became effective owing to lack of communications about the island and acute shortage of transport.

Next morning, Karlovasi had a third day of rejoicing; the bells rang out again in the church towers and the crackle of feux de joie broke the

BIGGER AND BETTER RAIDS

silence of the hills as Brigadier Turnbull, Commander, Raiding Forces, sailed up to the wharf in a Fairmile motor launch, bringing with him another score of Greek soldiers and some staff officers.

The local population turned out at once to give him an ovation, and with difficulty he pressed through the cheering crowd to the two elderly motor lorries, which were all the town could raise for the drive to Vathy.

The drive was a triumphal procession right across the island, every village or hamlet gathering to deck the Brigadier's party with flowers, offer them wine and fruit and here and there to insist upon an al fresco meal of fish, goat's milk cheese, rough bread, by then a luxury to the islanders, olives and wine. It was a great day for Samos.

The Brigadier drove into Vathy through ruined Pythagoreio, a small port, and there was a good bit of excitement and sporadic outbursts of wild applause when he appeared in the streets of the capital, although it had been decided to have the official rejoicing and a special ceremony on the following Sunday.

This was announced by the authorities and the peoples were asked to postpone all celebrations until then.

The Fascist Italian prisoners were housed in a tall, stone building facing the sea, and looked sadly onto former glory, while further parties were being brought in from time to time from their outposts.

Samos had been liberated without a single casualty. A great achievement and a triumph of propaganda, when the contrast in the size of forces is considered.

All that remained to do was to celebrate and the people of Samos did it. They praised God and Raiding Forces at a crowded service in the ornate and highly decorated main church of the island as they sang the "Te Deum" for liberation. Then a wreath was laid on the memorial in Vathy's main square, followed by an official banquet, at which the most remnants of the island's closely hoarded luxuries appeared.

The bloodless victory of Samos emphasises a very important part of the Raiding Forces' methods; all along they had been getting, and were still to get, the odd deserters from the enemy who felt that by and large the game was up and to whom the constant strain of fear had become intolerable: but here was the perfect example of unconditional surrender. A garrison comprising 1200 well-armed enemy troops, entrenched in strong prepared position had given in to a trifling Allied force because they were literally frightened for their lives of Raiding Forces.

All this, of course, was very tame stuff to the men of the unit, who revelled in the thrills and tension of a raid and who were, in the main, fire-eaters and proud of it. Their first phase of action after formation appears in the secret intelligence records under this very operation code name "Fire eater". But Force Headquarters and staff officers at G.H.Q. must have felt immensely gratified by the Samos incident. It was the general's dream so seldom realised in modern war of maximum gain with minimum of loss, in this case "Losses – Nil".

Samos was to be the only masterpiece of its kind in the Raiding Force annals; although the garrisons of Kos, Leros and Rhodes did surrender unconditionally on the day that Hitler's army was beaten to its knees in Germany itself. There were many other outstanding successes but nothing to equal that of the liberation of Samos.

No Escape

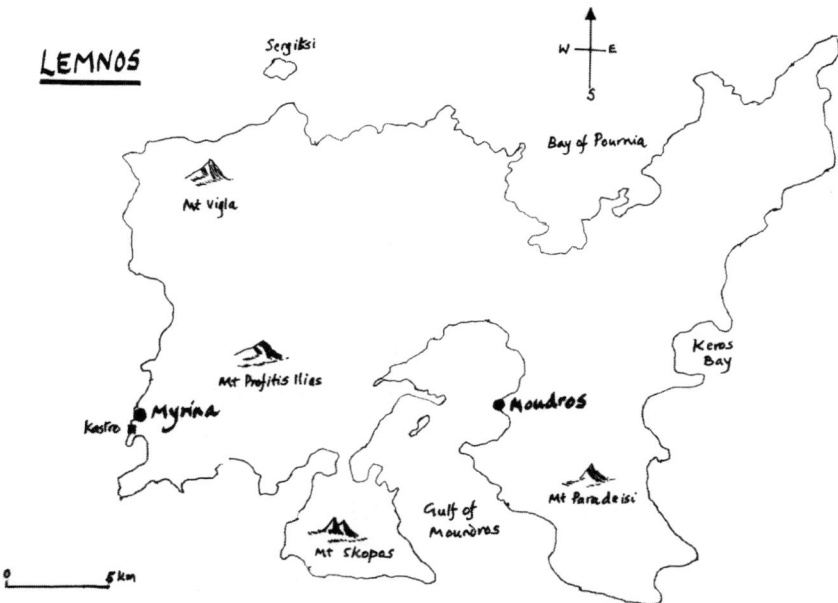

The next example of Phase Two is a sharp contrast to the liberation of Samos. The affray at Lemnos, from which the Germans hoped to evacuate their garrison intact, was crammed with action and the smell of powder.

High light of the attack took place on the wharf of Moudros, the island's chief garrison station, where two Allied Colonels, armed only with pistols, shot it out with a party of Germans attempting to escape in some caiques which were moored to the quay.

The Lemnos raid was made personally by the Commander, Raiding Forces, Brigadier Turnbull; his senior staff officer Lt-Col J. Neilson Lapraik, M.C., who had with him the Chief of Staff of the Greek Sacred Regiment, Lt-Col J. Roussos, was in command of the advance party of 75 officers and men who landed at Myrina, 20 miles from Moudros, in pouring rain, with no moon or stars to help them, a couple of hours before dawn on 16th October 1944.

The local Andartes met them, as had been previously arranged, on landing and then announced they had no transport. This entailed a forced march of 30 turn to Moudros, in the pitch dark and in pouring rain, along unfamiliar, muddy roads, carrying all the spare ammunition. Owing to the bad weather it took them six hours to make the trip.

At 08.00 hours, three hours later than they were expected, again due to the bad weather, the main body arrived. They had to get jeeps ashore, and the very devil of a job it proved. In the tossing sea, jeeps had to be manhandled from the ships to local lighters, and then landed from the lighters on to the beach. The final disaster to the time schedule was that the Germans had blown five bridges, every one of them impassable, on the road to Moudros but luckily as it turned out, not mined.

Colonel Lapraik, with the advance party, had dropped a couple of sovereigns at each of these points and arranged for emergency deviation work to be carried out.

Rough tracks were made, around which the jeeps, commanded by the Brigadier in person, and overloaded with men, could be taken. Meanwhile, the balance of the main party was to follow on foot.

The enthusiasm of the local Greeks was feverish and needed no urging. One village turned out every man, woman and child, and all worked feverishly, shifting great baulks of timber to make an impromptu bridge that later took quite comfortably a captured German three-tonner.

The advance party got to the outskirts of Moudros shortly before noon, and was joined by the jeeps with about 20 more men a little later. It was still, however, a very weak force for the attack and a delay was unavoidable until more troops arrived. Meanwhile the Germans could be seen to be pulling out of the bay and demolition charges were going off one after another.

A German E-boat that put out to sea suddenly turned and came back at speed because there was a British M.L. lying in wait just around the corner. At this point a Siebel ferry craft began to move away from the wharf and numbers of Germans, although they saw the E-boat put back, abandoned the shelter of buildings and walls to make a dash for the line of caiques and other small craft tied up alongside the wharf. A wild spirit of panic and "sauve qui peut" ran through the enemy troops although they had sufficient men to beat off an attack twice as strong as that put in by Raiding Forces.

This crazy rush for the boats was too much for the advance party who decided to take the risk and, few as they were, push boldly into the town.

One party rushed a Vickers gun down to the sea-front to sweep the wharf from the near end, while the remainder went straight through the houses and into the town prepared to tackle whatever they might meet.

They got as far as the dock area before they were opposed, and the two colonels who were well in front, came round the corner of a house to find a frantic mass of Germans frenziedly trying to get eleven caiques, that were ready to sail, away from the quayside before they could be boarded and captured.

Putting into action the Raiding Force motto "Who Dares Wins" they opened fire with their pistols at point blank range, while their bodyguards let drive with their automatic weapons. The sudden burst of fire, backed up by grenades which exploded in two of the caiques and set one of them on fire, delayed the enemy's escape for the short but vital period until the Vickers was in position. The blazing caique never left the stone quayside while another put off, having cut her moorings, with four limp bodies hanging over the side as she moved out into the bay.

With the flat clatter of a typewriter punched at speed, the Vickers got into action. A few seconds later two Bren guns were got into action from the gutters beside the wharf with a staccato chatter of short bursts, like riveters in a shipyard

The caiques divided. A group of five went westwards, pursued by the high-speed fire of the Vickers, while the other group made off towards the southwest, as the Brens opened up on them.

In the rear of the group was a caique, loaded until she was almost gunwale under fleeing Fascist Italians. The brutally accurate fire of the Brens, treating their ship as a woodpecker treats a rotten log was too much for them. Spinning the wheel hard over the helmsman ran the caique at full speed on to the shore, the frantic Italians jumping into the shallow water as she grounded and flinging their weapons away as they made for any kind of cover, only to be rounded up and put in the bag a short while later.

Meanwhile, the Vickers gun, from its position at the end of the quay was throwing belt after belt of ammunition into the gradually scattering group of caiques heading westwards towards the distant Greek mainland. The time was now just one o'clock and much has happened in the last hour.

The Siebel ferry, which had put to sea about the time that the E-boat turned back, had her full complement of about 150 men on board with another 150 German troops who wanted to escape as well. The ferry's armament consisted of two 88mm A.A. guns, two 81mm mortars and a number of 40mm and 20mm guns, which were being evacuated. Just before the caique "strafe" finished she decided to deal with the Allied shore party and thus give the caiques a chance to get clear. Closing in towards the shore, the Siebel ferry's commander waited until he was a bare 2,000 yards away and then opened fire on the three machine gun crews with a succession of air bursts from the 88s that made life more than a trifle unpleasant for the Britons and Greeks on the exposed waterfront. His two big mortars got into action as well and began lobbing their four inch bombs in a lazy arc into our positions. One dropped close to one of our mortars which was just getting into action and killed a Greek officer as well as wounding a member of the mortar crew.

Standing well up in Moudros was a high building that had been used as a German officers' mess. Knowing that it would make a good observation post the Siebel's skipper set his two 88s to range on it. Brigadier Turnbull and Colonel Lapraik had just come down from the roof where they had been spotting for our machine guns and mortars, when an 88mm shell hit where they had been standing an instant before and blew down most of the top storey.

Confident that its superior fire power had duly intimidated the raiders, the Siebel ferry carefully came further in short and began to try and take in tow a large German fuel lighter lying in the bay with cables out ready to be got out. As soon as the ferry was within 1500 yards of the shore, the Vickers crew showed what could be done with a high-speed precision weapon. They swept the Siebel's deck and lived to talk of the ghastly accuracy of our machine gunners.

While the Germans' attention was fully occupied by the shambles on the ferry's bloodstained deck, our mortars had got into action and were plastering the loaded fuel lighter with their bombs and set it on fire. Forty-eight hours later it was still burning, an almost gutted hulk, but a tribute to our men's brilliant shooting.

Seeing the fuel lighter burst into flames the mortar crews switched targets and a few seconds later landed two bombs on the Siebel's deck, adding to the casualties and confusion caused by our M.G. fire and doing some more damage.

Despite her colossal superiority in armament, the Siebel ferry was licked and abandoned the fight, putting out to sea at top speed. Another Siebel ferry had escaped from Moudros the night before Raiding Forces' pre-dawn landing, but despite the almost zero visibility cause by the heavy rain on a moonless night she was intercepted and sunk by a British cruiser.

Seeing the gun flashes of this brief action had heartened our men when they landed on the island of Lemnos. The other Siebel ferry, which is believed to have escaped safely, was later discovered to have had the German Naval port commander, Richthofen, aboard. He was a cousin of the famous German airman of World War I, the Ritter von Richthofen, of air circus fame.

With no more ships and caiques to attack, the Raiding Force party turned its attention to the town of Moudros. Although the town itself was of little or no importance, the German demolitions displayed typical Hun thoroughness. The few buildings in which no charges had been set were as badly damaged by shock and blast as those which had been destroyed by delayed explosive charges.

The real value of Moudros to either side lay in its dock and harbour facilities which are best described as being like a smaller edition of the

British Naval installations at Scapa Flow. Moudros possessed a first-class seaplane base, excellent equipment and adequate quarters and offices. All the buildings were solidly constructed of local stone. The garrison had done itself extremely well too, as the raiding party found when they reached the ration store. This was captured intact, with fruit, all kinds of tinned delicacies and even a quantity of 1941 vintage German hock. Although the Greek population on all the enemy occupied islands was nearing starvation and showed definite evidence of malnutrition, the German garrisons lacked nothing in the way of luxuries.

Shortly after the action finished the troops were withdrawn from the town area and took up a position on the hills, because of the large number of delayed action charges left by the Germans. As dusk fell, at about six o'clock in the evening, the ammunition dump went up, sending a great column of smoke into the sky, which spread slowly into a great black umbrella that hung over the site at a height of about 600 feet.

Next day the sappers, guided by an English-speaking Austrian, defused the delayed charges that had not yet exploded and it was possible to take an inventory of the war material that had fallen into the hands of Raiding Forces. It included 20 field telephone sets, that the men of Raiding Forces Signals considered preferable to our own issue and put to excellent use in subsequent operations against the Hun. Another acquisition, although rather too big for operational use on raids, was a hundred-line telephone exchange which fell into our hands intact and proved a valuable piece of salvage.

An important factor in the resumption of civil work, for the benefit of Greece as a whole, on Lemnos, was the fat that although the beaches were heavily mined, there were very few inland minefields to interfere with agriculture.

Lemnos had had 6,000 Germans in the garrison on it at one time; working with the frantic industry of moles they had hollowed nearly every hill and enlarged and linked together the many caves to be used as storehouses and dumps. The strategic role of Lemnos was to be an air and sea base if Turkey entered the war on the Allies' side.

NO ESCAPE

Twenty-four hours after they had landed, our troops began to collect the Nazis who had escaped to the hills. They garnered 75 on the first day and then went after the balance of the garrison, about 50 men, who were still hiding. These included the German Engineer officer who had arranged the demolitions, whom the island community were particularly anxious to get hold of. He had a remarkable unsavoury reputation as far as the local women were concerned and the Greeks wished to try him on a number of charges of rape.

Suggesting that the German always behaves in the same manner wherever he may be is the story of a German atrocity on Lemnos, which is on a par with what happened at Belsen and Buchenwald. A certain Greek was arrested for voicing an opinion about the German Gestapo's behaviour on the island. As a punishment for talking out of turn he was put into a cell, soaked in petrol and set alight.

Having survived this ghastly treatment, he was later hauled out of his cell, his burns being left untended, and flung into another cell. He lay in almost unbelievable pain for a week. Then he was taken back to Myrina where he had been arrested, and his mutilated and dying body flung on the ground in the town as an awful warning to the citizens of what even vocal opposition to the Nazi regime would lead to.

Another story relates to the German commandant who, when drunk, would start a shooting match, the target being the ceiling of his billet, although his unwilling civilian hosts had to sleep upstairs. The age-old German hobby of looting was also practised on a large scale; anything that took the fancy of a member of the Nazi garrison was taken by him as a matter of course. Even trifles like salt cellars and pepper pots were stolen from civilian homes to be used in the German messes.

The population of Lemnos became almost hysterical with joy when the island was cleared and the last of the despised and hated Germans captured. Women and children wept and everybody from bearded grandfathers downwards seized any soldier, British or Greek, they could get near and kissed him heartily on both cheeks. The graceful and traditional Greek island custom of handing nosegays, bouquets of flowers or bunches of fragrant, scented, basil and thyme and other herbs to those towards whom the islanders want to show their affection resulted in every man of the Raiding Forces going round the countryside and towns with armfuls of flowers. As a soldier walked through the streets, or down the roads, his fragrant bundle grew every time he passed a house. Girl after girl would add her tribute from the home garden to the soldier's ever-growing load, while the jeeps looked like mobile, inhabited flowerbeds.

Myrina, the only town of any size on Lemnos, is not unlike a Fife fishing village with its trim, clean cottages and masses of fresh, clean, herb-scented house-linen, for the island women, like the Scots, are vastly house-proud.

It was almost impossible for the troops to eat their own rations, so much hospitality was thrust upon them. As on all the Greek islands, the food was plain and simple: goat's milk cheese, eggs, honey, chickens and the pleasant local wine. So keen were the people to entertain their liberators that there was considerable competition to get a British officer to stay for a night with them.

After the last German was captured and the last delayed action charge had been removed the men of Raiding Forces returned to Myrina, leaving a troop of the Greek Sacred Regiment as garrison at Moudros.

In Moudros they held a simple service for those who had fallen freeing Lemnos at the Greek cemetery and buried them in the plot next to those who fell in the 1914-18 war, whose graves had been neglected by German orders, during the occupation.

The Last Shots

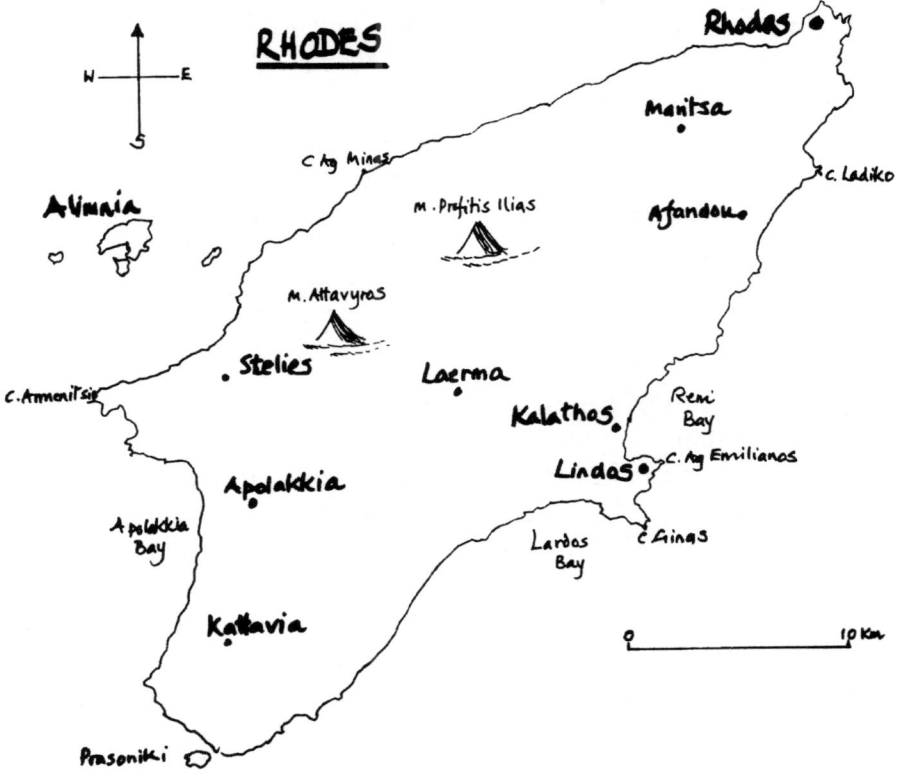

On May 2nd, 1945, barely a week before the German surrender in Europe, came the last full-scale operation, a lightning attack on Rhodes and its satellite island, Alimnia, with a force of 180 all ranks commanded by Lt-Col Lapraik, MC.

The whole raid was completed in six hours, everything went like clockwork.

Rhodes was garrisoned by about 10,000 Germans and Italians altogether, but the attack was planned to hit and run before the reserves could be rushed to the threatened area, and was a good example of the military paradox of striking, with greater strength than the enemy, even when he greatly outnumbers you.

TERROR BY NIGHT

The actual garrisons attacked were estimated to be 40 men and a 105mm and two 88mm guns at Chimarasse; four and eight men respectively at Foca and Stelies, two points close together with a telephone between them, who had a 75mm self-propelled gun and a truck and were responsible for manning an O.P.

At Noti there were four men armed with rifles, to control the fishing boats, they also had a telephone as well as a dog for the night watch; Vunara was scheduled to have a strong garrison, but a recent report said it was now held by only 12 men, with an 88mm self-propelled gun and two light machine guns. Alimnia, the satellite island, just off the coast, had 20 men distributed at strong-points and a 75mm gun. All the strong-points on both islands were well protected by minefields and heavy barbed wire defences.

The enemy reserves against raids and invasion were formidable. A complete battalion of motorised infantry, with four tanks and four 75mm field guns were posted at Laerma, only 20 miles from Vunara, one of the points to be attacked. This highly mobile reserve could have got there in less than hour after receiving the alarm. A further reserve was stationed at Apolakkia with seven trucks and a staff car, and estimated to consist of anything from 60 to 150 men. The real menace at Apolakkia for the raiders came from a pair of guns each with a range of 20,800 yards which were able to put down fire on all the landing beaches to be used.

There were also two 75s, three 88s and two 105mm guns near Angonia which could also cover our landing and a large calibre gun at Kattavia site to engage the beaches south of Noti. Yet another mobile reserve, of 600 men with two mobile 88s and two field guns was known to be held at Apollona, but it was decided that they were just too far away from the nearest of our objectives to be able to move up before we had got clear.

The training for this last, big operation had been gruelling. The country was mountainous, everybody had to be fighting fit and even the old sweats at the game were given fresh training described as "energetic and vigorous in the extreme". Marches over rough country with full loads by night, rock and hill climbing by night, and repeated practice of the complete assault drill were embodied in the training.

Firing practices with light machine guns, tommy guns, carbines, pistols

THE LAST SHOTS

and grenades were gone through every day in addition to the night practices.

Nineteen foolscap pages and four specially drawn maps were included in the orders which covered only three hours' work, but the ultimate result justified it.

The operation report of the landings, in its usual laconic style, by the officer in charge, gives a clear picture of all that went on at each beach.

"Chimarasse force: After receiving the signal from the shore the force landed at 21.45 hours, 1st May, and received the latest information from the advanced patrol. The force then moved off towards the Chimarasse plateau, leaving the mortar section on top of the cliffs about 200 yards from the beach.

"By 00.15 hours, 2nd May, all troops were ready in position for assault. Possible escape routes were covered, and arrangements made to cut the telephone wires. The main assault was from the south of the enemy positions.

"Two troops attacked at 00.30 hours with light machine guns, tommy guns and grenades. Tents, ammunition and hutments were early set on fire, and an unknown number of the enemy was burned to death in these fires. The position was cleared by 00.45 hours, and one troop sent back to the beach with prisoners of war and our one wounded man.

"The remaining troop consolidated its position, while the British Royal Engineers carried out demolitions, which were completed by 01.35 hours, when all forces commenced to withdraw. At 02.00 hours, the mortar section opened fire on the rear of Chimarasse position, spreading fire over as large an area as possible, to discourage enemy reinforcements.

"All troops had returned to the beach by 02.45 hours and the embarkation of Chimarasse and Foca parties began as soon as prisoners of war and our own wounded were aboard. All forces were on the motor launches by 03.25 hours."

The known results here were: twelve enemy killed and twelve taken prisoners.

The remainder, including some wounded, escaped. Four 88mm guns and trailers, 6 light machine guns, a wireless truck, all tents, stores, hutments and ammunition were destroyed by fire and demolition. Our own casualties were one man wounded.

"Foca: The Force landed here at 21.45 hours, 1st May, and had to make a forced march to its objectives owing to the landing being a little late. The Force was in position by 00.35 hours, 2nd May, and attacked immediately.

The positions were cleared within ten minutes. Tents and hutments were set on fire and demolitions were begun under cover of one section. The Force withdrew to the beach by 02.45 hours and were picked up with the Chimarasse Force."

Results at Foca: nine enemy killed and 5 captured, while one armoured car, one command vehicle, four light machine guns and all the tents, stores and hutments were destroyed. Our own casualties were nil.

"Noti: The signal was received from the beach, and the Force completed its landing by 22.55 hours, 1st May, after a very quick disembarkation, as the landing was much behind schedule. The Force then split into two parties, one for Noti and one for Vunara, and made forced marches to the targets.

"The Vunara party was in the target areas by 02.00 hours, 2nd May, and as time did not permit of positions to be taken up, the Force approached the target, making use of cover.

"The party was challenged by a sentry, who was killed. Thereafter the Force went in with tommy guns and grenades, and cleared the position in ten minutes. Under cover of one section, the engineers completed their demolitions, and finally everybody left the position by 01.00 hour, reaching the beach at 01.45 hours. Here it met with Noti party, which had had a similar success and both embarked by 03.00 hours."

Results of these two jobs were three enemy killed and 13 made prisoners, two men, one of them wounded, escaped, but our patrols destroyed an armoured car, 3 light machine guns, as well as the telephone equipment and the tents, stores and hutments. This operation cost us two wounded.

Alimnia Episode

"An M.L. took us to the bay where our particular landing-beach was," said Capt. R.N.C. France. "Everything went according to plan, and the landing was accomplished without difficulty."

His party, commanded by Major Kiriakos Papageorgopoulos, paddled ashore in rubber boats. By midnight they had scaled the rocks and moved more than a mile inland. Some of the men were carrying seventy-pound loads of explosives.

A whispered order from the Major sent a small detachment with a PIAT gun down to a narrow inlet where a German EMS craft – one of the principle targets – was hiding up.

One of the Greeks dropped out the main party. He swarmed a telegraph pole at the side of the track, and slashed down the wires.

HQ was sited on a promontory overlooking the objectives. The moon, which could have betrayed the raiding force's movements rose when they were already lying flat amongst the boulders and patches of mint waiting to strike.

By 0005 hours, 2nd May, all parties were in position. With HQ were MMGs and mortars. Another detachment – the main one – were waiting to attack in quick succession two machine-gun posts in the enemy's chief positions.

"Shortly after we had sited the HQ mortars, we heard gun-fire miles down the coast," Capt. France said. "It was diversionary fire from a destroyer to distract attention from our area. We just lay where we were and waited. There was still half an hour to go before zero hour."

At 0045 hours precisely the EMS craft was rocked by the first PIAT bomb. The attack had begun. Not only on Alimnia, but away across on the Rhodes coast the tracer could be seen. The night sky was lit with the sudden flare of explosions, the steady red of fires.

The EMS craft, pounded by the PIAT, had caught fire. Yelling Germans dived overboard to swim ashore and surrender.

"It was like a Brooks firework show," Cpl John Garvey said. "I saw the gun-boat going up in a shower of sparks and ammo, bursting red and green, with oil blazing on the water.

"It wasn't my show – I was just coming away from putting a charge on a petrol dump – but my path back up the hill was more like an illuminated fairyland. And I could hear Germans across the stretch of water where the EMS craft lay – they were bawling 'Kamerad' at the top of their voices."

Meanwhile, the main party had attacked and reduced the enemy's main position and his machine guns. The remaining Germans were attacked with all arms but without complete success. They were well dug-in, well-armed, and full of resistance.

Time did not permit a further assault. Eight of the enemy had been killed, twenty-seven captures; tents, weapons, equipment, and supplies had been destroyed. The German gun-boat was a blazing hulk.

The raiders withdrew to an alternative beach, taking their prisoners with them. These were a mixed bag of Italians and Germans, some of whom had been dragged from their beds, and were now wrapped in blankets.

By 0325 hours the embarkation was complete.

This raid was an outstanding success – in the words of the Raiding Force G.I. "very nearly the 'complete' raid". He reported further:

"The whole op. went off almost entirely to plan. Heavy casualties were inflicted on the enemy, both in men and material, as against our own casualties of five wounded, one of them only slightly. Co-operation between the Navy and Raiding Forces was outstanding, and a fitting conclusion to the saga of Dodecanese ops.

"B. Squadron of the Greek Sacred Regiment showed considerable dash on this, its first big-scale operation. A. Squadron's performance was worthy of the Squadron's traditions. In particularly, Major Papageorgopoulos, Commander of the Alimnia force, showed leadership and gallantry of a high order in what turned out to be by far the hardest attack of the night.

"Raiding Force Signals, were, as usual, first class."

Parade "Dismiss"

Although, throughout the last phase, the Raiding Forces operations seemed to become increasingly spectacular, there was still the same meticulous planning before each patrol went out to continue the clearing of the Aegean islands of their temporary Nazi tenants. They kept up a steady pressure of demolitions, minor attacks and death in the night until the nervous strain on the isolated enemy commanders must have been terrific.

It was quite clear that the end was very close in Europe, but Brigadier Turnbull very wisely kept up the safety regulations against incurring casualties and instead of making a spectacular all-out assault, without regard for casualties, as many a lesser commander would have done, the final major operation – on Rhodes – was carried through with the same economical regard for the lives of his men that he had displayed throughout the entire 22 months of glorious, even though unpublicised, achievement.

As a result, the simultaneous twin raids on Rhodes and its satellite island, Alinnia, increased the prestige of Raiding Forces, much more greatly, by the low casualty price of success, than a more spectacular show in which a trail of blood marked the path of the unit to victory.

By the time the Nazis gave in in Europe, the islands were mostly free. The Huns in Crete were virtually prisoners and the small territory still in German hands was relatively unimportant, as time was bringing the occupation to a close inevitably; what gain there was in capturing Rhodes, Kos, and Leros did not warrant the risk of casualties. Shortage of supplies was doing the work of an assault and the enemy's teeth had been drawn. As far as our war effort was concerned, the German invader in the Aegean was harmless.

To prevent the Axis troops plucking up their courage for a "death and glory" suicide assault on some vital Allied installation in the Japanese manner, the nervous tension was kept up by small raids until the eve of V-E day. On the day following the third Reich's unconditional surrender, the few remaining Nazi island garrisons gave in.

TERROR BY NIGHT

The limelight of surrender was on Rhodes, to police which a force of ordinary troops had been waiting on a nearby island since early in the year. Many of its personnel had never heard a shot fired in action and it was with eyes of envy that they watched the men of Raiding Forces go off to fight an enemy that they would never see till he surrendered.

When the fighting finished in the field, Raiding Forces concentrated all resources on another war they had been waging since they first arrived. It was a battle against starvation and it had been going on since the first raiding patrols saw the plight of the islanders. Time after time a patrol landing on an occupied island had also landed several tons of food and medical supplies for the hardy men and women who, with a negligible percentage of Quislings among them, had guarded the raiders' secrets as if they were their own.

Instead of marching silently by night in their rubber-soled parachute boots and landing from Naval small craft under cover of the dark, the British and Greek patrols were seen by day on the roads with no attempt at concealment.

They were seeing that the food and other supplies landed on the islands got into the right people's hands. Raiding Forces were ensuring that there would be no black market in the goods sent in to combat the ravages of malnutrition.

Our men were known and trusted by all classes of the Greek population and feared for the relentless certainty of their revenge, by many of the Italian settlers. These peoples' minds had inclined to betraying the invaders, particularly if they were friends to the Gestapo in war and could reasonably be relied on to start black market rackets now that peace had arrived.

For this reason, no better force could have been chosen for food administration until UNRRA personnel were allowed to land and take over the job.

The last scene in the crowded, short, life of Brigadier Turnbull's command was the most spectacular; the transformation scheme of the Christmas pantomime played before an audience of thousands.

The lean, bearded men, whose strictly utilitarian clothing and ever-

PARADE "DISMISS"

present weapons, had emphasised the operational role of Raiding Forces, become polished soldiers overnight.

As they marched onto the vast green playing field of the El Alamein Club, Cairo, heads back and chests out, it was like watching a ceremonial parade at home in peacetime.

With khaki drill shirts and shorts, starched until they could have stood up without a man inside, blancoed belts and brasses gleaming in the sun, they waited, 1,000 strong, to be inspected by the Commander-in-Chief, of the Middle East Forces, General Sir Bernard Paget.

On parade were the men of the R.F. Headquarters Squadron, together with the Royal Engineers, Royal Corps of Signals and the R.E.M.E., Floating Light Recovery Section, all that was left of the British personnel of the unit. The others had left, starting with the L.R.D.G., in the early summer of 1944, to become the mainstay of Land Forces, Adriatic. After the L.R.D.G., had followed the Special Boat Service and the Raiding Support Regiment a few months later, while the Kalpaks had been disbanded.

But to make up for absent friends the men of the Greek Sacred Regiment were there at full strength. Their commander, Colonel T. Tsigantes had led them since the Sacred Squadron was formed in the black summer before the battle of El Alamein, from the nucleus of 120 officers who had escaped from Greece and revived a unit from history.

Their numbers had been increased in October 1943 to 350, when private soldiers and N.C.Os were allowed to volunteer for the Regiment, subsequently the numbers were increased to 1,100.

Behind the main parade, were parties dressed in the operational clothing worn in their specialist roles. Nothing could have shown the crowd, of 4,000 civilians who came to cheer, the powers of endurance brought out in these men by hard training.

Wearing the winter clothing of ski-troops and mountain warfare experts they paraded for two hours under Cairo's midsummer sun, while the onlookers sweated in thin frocks or shorts and shirts. With these men on the parade were others in parachute jumping suits, and the watertight rubber suits worn in Folboats.

TERROR BY NIGHT

In spite of the heat these men stood as rigidly as the rest and marched past the saluting base as smartly.

Addressing the Unit after he had inspected them, General Paget said:

"Brigadier Turnbull, officers and men of Raiding Forces, I am glad indeed to have this opportunity of meeting you before you disperse, and of expressing to you my high appreciation of the work you have done for the Allied cause.

"The success of your operations can be measured by the greatly superior enemy forces which you contained, thereby setting free Allied forces and Allied shipping for employment in the main theatre.

"Your achievements bear witness to the fine leadership, skill and courage of all concerned.

"To the officers and men of the Greek Sacred Regiment, I say, you have a proud tradition, and you have proved yourselves worthy of your motor, "Victory or Death". Over 2,000 years ago the first Sacred Regiment established that motto and died to save These from the Spartans: 120 years ago the second Sacred Regiment did likewise and preferred death to surrender.

"You of the third Sacred Regiment formed in September 1941, will return to your homes as victors: and I hope you will always remember the great tradition which, as members of the Sacred Regiment, you have inherited and that you will always uphold it, the tradition of fearless and unselfish devotion to the service of your country.

"It is fitting that this farewell parade should take place here, in the Middle East, where the first squadron of the Sacred Regiment was formed three years ago, and, during its time with the Eighth Army, under General Leclerc, and later under General Freyburg, gained great distinction and suffered heavy casualties.

"Then, after a period of intensive training, you began operations against the enemy in Greece, when, led by your distinguished Commander, Colonel Tsigantes, you dropped by parachute on Samos. There followed your bold and successful raids on Khios, on Mitilini, on Amorgos and on Symi. Your work, in the words of an officer of the Sacred Regiment, consisted in 'making life miserable for the Germans, and that you did very thoroughly.

PARADE "DISMISS"

"Also, the accurate information which you provided about the enemy was of great value. It enabled us to harass the Germans in their withdrawal from the Greek islands, and, later, to pin down those left in the Dodecanese. Most recently the capture of Tilos and your last raid on Rhodes made a fitting climax to your victorious history.

"There can be few, if any, units in the Allied forces who have caused more casualties and damage to the enemy than Raiding Forces, since they were first formed in October 1943, after the withdrawal from Kos and Leros: and there can be few, if any, units with wider or more varied experience. I wish to make a special mention of Raiding Force Signals in this connection; they have done splendid work and have contributed much to the success of the many operations in which they have taken part. Also the R.E.M.E. section which included a floating workshop; and the Royal Engineers.

"And the story of your endeavours would not be complete without paying a very high tribute to the co-operation of the Royal Navy and to the Royal Air Force in the achievements of Raiding Forces.

"Now Raiding Forces will pass into history and you will disperse, some to continue as soldiers and others to return to civil life. But wherever you go and whatever you do, the spirit of Raiding Forces will live on and you will always have with you that sense of true comradeship which comes of dangers and hardships shared in the common cause.

"And most important of all are the enduring ties of friendship which have been established in Raiding Forces between our gallant Allies, the Greeks, and ourselves.

"I wish you all good fortune and God speed."

There was a brief pause after General Paget had finished speaking and the four score newspaper reporters in the Press Stand finished their notes. Commendation of a unit in terms of such instituted praise is rare and much less praise is usually followed by sour comments on "luck" from other units.

In this case the large crowd of guests and onlookers cheered Raiding Forces to the echo. No one grudged praise of a unit whose performance had been so outstanding.

TERROR BY NIGHT

A few moments later the cheers were returned with interest, by the men on parade, after Brigadier Turnbull had given the order "Caps off – Three cheers for the Commander-in-Chief". British "hurrahs" mingled with the "Zitos" of the Greeks as the combined roar of their shouts echoed across the Nile.

Their Royal Highnesses Crown Prince Paul and Princess Frederica of Greece, the Commander-in-Chief, the high staff officers from G.H.Q., and the British and Greek ministers left, a crowd of lesser guests and spectators eddying past the official cars with their pennants.

The vast oval of vivid green grass, surrounded by empty stands seemed to be double the size it had been a few minutes previously as small groups of soldiers from Britain and Greece exchanged impressions of the first and last parade of Raiding Forces.

Lasting friendships had been formed between the fighting men of Britain and Greece, cemented by dangers shared and a mutual appreciation of each other's virtues. As long as any man who fought in the Aegean lives, there will be men in both countries determined to see that no country or man shall cause a break between Britain and Greece.

In a few weeks, the last men could have left and no city would see again the happy parties of Raiding Forces men, tasting the luxuries of civilisation after cramped months at sea in caiques or hiding far behind the Nazi lines making notes of all that went on.

The beige beret and the flat-topped parachute wings would no longer be seen in the Middle East. The Greek Sacred Regiment was disbanding, for the first time in over 2,000 years. Formed only in times of national emergency, so grave that death in the field must be the sole alternative to victory, this third unit to bear the wreathed sword badge was the first one to achieve its aim. Both its predecessors had died to a man but these would return home as victors.

The ghosts of the first Sacred Squadron, who died fighting before Thebes against the Spartans in 370 B.C., must have watched the various ceremonies of disbandment with pride – the torch of freedom, lighted in the plains of Achaia 2,300 years ago burned yet more brightly today.

Spread through the Greek Army, in units of all kinds, according to the

PARADE "DISMISS"

arm of service from which they came, the officers and men of the Sacred Regiment will spread its ideals through a larger sphere.

Freedom and democracy can only be helped, not hindered, by the application of the motto of the original SAS Regiment, of whom the SBS, and HQ RF were a part – the motto which was carried on, after the other units had left, by Raiding Forces – "Who Dares Wins".

To the British personnel, who had left their mark in the hearts of the island Greeks for all time, the parade meant a number of different things. The men who had been in the Middle East since the early desert battles were being repatriated under the "Python" scheme.

At home they would meet the other men of Raiding Forces who had missed the celebration because their overseas term of duty had expired before the final defeat of the enemy.

With them would leave the older men who had been in the army since the outbreak of war, demobilisation called them back to the civil life they had half forgotten.

Watching them pack for home were three other groups whose future was unlikely to prove as exciting as the past. Some of them were to join units fighting in the Far East against Japan, others to technical appointments for which their Raiding Force experience qualified them and the rest, who had only seen short service in the Middle East theatre of war, to fill vacancies in garrison units that had been caused by the ravages of demobilisation.

Wherever they go, one picture will always linger in their minds to link them with the Aegean, 1943-1945.

They will see again the eve of a raid. The crowded base caique gaily tricked out in bright red, blue, green and other coloured paints to hide her scars. On the deck a patrol in oddly assorted clothes preparing their packs and weapons and getting ready to move off.

A little conference of officers with maps on the high poop deck is going over the plans for the last time, while between the two groups the gallant Greek crew, from skipper to cook's boy are getting a last hot meal ready for the raiders, without a thought of the inevitable torture and execution facing them if they were caught by the enemy.

TERROR BY NIGHT

Whether the ship he lived on was the Agios Georgios, the Towfik, or another, no man, who ever saw the dawn light up the mountains and rock of an Aegean island while waiting for the attack, can forget the good fellowship under primitive conditions that existed between all ranks.

If ever the picture fades slightly the music of "Pistol Packin' Momma", the song of the Raiders in the summer of 1944, will make the focus sharp again.

Farewell men of Raiding Forces, last inheritors of the great Elizabethan spirit.

END

We Pay a Debt

This book could not have been written and its detailed guaranteed accurate but for the great help extended this department by the Commander, officers and men of Raiding Forces, and officers and men of the Royal Navy.

Our thanks are due to:-

Brigadier D.J.T. Turnbull, C.B.E., D.S.O., Commander Raiding Forces, for making available his records and reports.

Major O'Shaughnessy and other officers and Sgt. E. Norton and Sgt. H. Verrier of Raiding Forces for the way they provided detailed information, answered questions and verified facts at all hours of the twenty-four.

Lieut-Commander James Morgan, R.N.V.R., Lieut. Frank Coulter, S.A.N.(V) and other officers and men of the Royal Navy who carried us to various islands and on various raids and gave up their sleep to keep us in the picture and see our information was accurate.

Cpl. Zena Neate, A.T.S. who produced the original typescript from the rough pen and ink slips and put in many hours of overtime to ensure that the manuscript reached the printers on time.

Finally, and most sincerely, to all the officers and men of Raiding Forces, afloat and ashore in the Aegean, for the way they instructed us up there, took us raiding and instilled into us their own vivid enthusiasm for the sport.

To all who hunted the Axis, by land and sea in the Aegean, this book is dedicated in the hope that it will cause their work up there to be more widely appreciated.

| "Fritz" Read, Captain. | Walter Warden U.D.F., Captain | J.A.G. Long, Captain. |
| Chief Observer Officer. | Observer Officer. | Observer Officer. |

No. 1 Public Relations Service,
G.H.Q., M.E.F.,
July 1945.
502/GDC – 7/45

Appendix "A"

Boarders Away

By Lieut. F.NB. Coulter, S.A.N.(V).

At 1800 hours on a day in June 1944 – two hours before dusk – the crew of our seventy-foot motor launch turned to. The gunners tested and loaded the guns, while others attended to the life boat, floats and the numerous other things which require attention before putting to see.

The Commanding Officer, First Lieutenant and an Army Captain were in the charthouse – the chart table piled with charts, maps, signals and recce photos. They were discussing the plan of operations for the night.

Certain enemy shipping movements had been reported to us by signal, and our object was to intercept, sink or board the enemy vessels. The discovery and passing on of the information regarding enemy shipping movements was the responsibility of Raiding Force recce parties and it was very seldom that they did not get the exact time of departure and destination of the enemy which made things a great deal easier for us.

Our crew comprised 2 Officers and 10 Ratings. In addition, we carried one British Army Captain, one Greek interpreter and about ten Army O.R.s who were used for boarding parties. These soldiers were armed with sub-machine guns, hand grenades and Lewis bombs, the latter being used for destroying the boarded ship if it was of no value to us.

On this particular day, we had received news of six caiques escorted by three armed caiques and one trawler, moving from North to South.

Before proceeding any further, I would like to mention that the caiques were manned by Greek crews who were pro-British, but they were German controlled and forced to carry three to four German guards; one of these guards was usually on watch while the rest slept. I am quite certain that the Germans had no knowledge or previous experience of the sea; most of those whom we saw were very sea sick and had no idea of their position. Often I have picked up a stray caique manned by a Greek crew, bluffing the German guards as to their whereabouts while endeavouring to contact a British ship or hideout to whom they could give themselves up.

However, to proceed with the story. Boarding ships or caiques is not an easy operation. There are many snags. We naturally preferred dark nights, but encountered difficulties in picking up the target. The course and speed of enemy shipping could only be estimated, as also the type of armament on escorting vessels for caiques carrying either troops or food. Lastly, we had to manoeuvre into a position so that we could creep up unobserved astern of the enemy convoy. This was down by lying close inshore, or against some out-jutting rock, waiting for the enemy convoy to pass.

On most occasions our engines were cut and we did not drift far, but in rather rough weather our engines were kept running and we had to rely on the lap of waves inshore to drown the drone of our main motors. The enemy convoys could be heard from some considerable distance due to the fact that the large majority of caiques and schooners are fitted with one or two cylinder engines but no silencer, which consequently make a noise rather resembling a steam train. (These caiques were fondly known among the British crews as "Chuff-chuffs".) In most cases red sparks could also be seen being discharged from the exhaust pipe.

On this particular night, we slipped silently from a little cove in an enemy unoccupied island where we had been lying for a few days. The weather was fine and the night promised to be dark. Our destination was a cover some ten miles from our hideout; we knew the route of the convoy and it was our intention to lie in wait until the convoy arrived at that particular point. If the convoy, for some reason, did not arrive, we were to return to our hideout one hour before daylight.

At approximately 2200 hours the lookout reported engine noise in a northly direction. The alarm was given. Gun crews and boarding parties closed up to their respective stations. Everything was very orderly. No panic. No fuss. Remember, the crews and boarding parties were trained men. There was an air of tenseness and excitement, as we waited for what seemed hours. We knew only too well what odds were piled against us but we also knew that if we worked fast and efficiently we could pull it off, with surprise as our greatest weapon. We could not afford to make

TERROR BY NIGHT

blunders; too much was at stake.

At 2230 hours the lookout reported six objects on the starboard bow which we presumed to be the enemy convoy. Shortly afterwards, this was confirmed. We could see no signs of their escorting vessels but this was not unusual as it was customary for escorts to sail to seaward, thus enabling their convoy to travel close inshore, where, it was hoped, they would be less conspicuous with the land as background. We waited for approximately thirty minutes for the caiques to sail past. They were about five hundred yards from us and we estimated their speed to be between four and five knots. We saw no movement on the upper decks with the exception of the Greek crew manning the helm. We could not have wished for anything better.

Silently we crept up astern of the last caique; the boarding party clinging to the guard rails, tommy guns at the alert, waiting for the order to board. Every man had his special job to do and the grim expressions on their faces as they crouched there left no doubts that the jobs would be done well. Gradually we sailed closer until the bows of our ship were touching the stern of the caique which we had selected as our first objective.

So far as we knew we had not been observed. All this time our forward guns were trained on the Greek helmsmen. Everything was perfect and working according to plan. I swung my ship to starboard and then hard to port, coming alongside the caique slightly forward to amidships. By this time the boarding party were over and had silenced the four German guards and within a few minutes had taken full control of the caique, without firing a shot or attracting the attention of the remaining ships in the convoy.

Our next job was to get our "prize" to safety and then go after the remainder. As in all sports, one "win" only made us more eager for another, but this time we were to be unlucky. Our caique developed engine trouble after we had towed her to moderate safety and we could not leave her with only two of the boarding party as was our usual practice. We had no option but to tow her to a safe anchorage. By the time this was completed, we had lost the remainder of the convoy. The following day we had time to look over our prize capture. She was a caique of 250 tons, Greek owned and newly built in Salonika but, much to our disgust, she had just discharged her cargo. However, we were well satisfied with our night's effort. That evening, with a "Prize Crew" on board (a Naval Coxswain and two of the Army boarding party) we sailed her to Kastellorizo, our nearest and then the only British-held island in the Aegean.

This is, of necessity, only a short episode of one of the many boarding operations carried out in the Aegean. There have been times when one of our small ships have boarded and captured three or four ships in one convoy at a time. I cannot imagine what explanation the Commanding Officer of the Enemy Escorts gave to his superior officers when he arrived at his destination on some occasions with as many as four caiques missing! In my opinion, I think it took until very nearly the end of the Aegean war before the Germans realised exactly how it was done.

I cannot give any definite figures as to the number of caiques captured, or wrecked, but I can assure you our small flotilla, with the aid of Raiding Forces dealt with a good many.

Appendix "B"

Andartes in the Islands

The rough, scrub covered, rocky hills of the Aegean islands make good cover for guerrilla troops. Roads suitable for motor transport are few and the stony tracks across the mountains give the lightly clad and sure-footed Greek a big advantage over the more clumsy German.

But despite the advantages of striking from cover, in a friendly country, against a hated foe and with the certainty that most of the people would risk their lives to help them escape, the Greek Andartes were a great disappointment. Only on certain occasions were they of real help.

On the principle that anyone who was against the Axis should be helped, the Allies had taken great risks to arm the Andartes, but when it came to doing an operation, the fatal spirit of "later, later" cropped up among them.

When Raiding Forces dealt with the Axis troops on Lemnos, 500 Andartes came charging into Mudhros long after the battle was over, and were very disappointed by the town's people refusing to provide them with food and wine, for a celebration. This kind of attempt to cash in on a victory, by men who had not fought, happened in many places.

On another operation, the Andartes promised guides and nine mules to be waiting for an Allied patrol landing on a lonely beach. The raiders got ashore and found no one there. Burdened with the loads for the mules, which included food, mortars and mortar bombs and other supplies they could only get a couple of miles from the beach before the imminence of dawn made them cache the supplies and hide up for the day.

At nine o'clock the following night, when the Anglo-Greek party had buried all they could not carry on their backs, two men turned up, each with one mule. They explained that the rest had decided the enterprise did not interest them.

At the mere fact of being a day late they grinned – what was a day more or less. The problems of time, distance and arriving punctually at the departure beach left them unmoved. In many cases it was due to sheer simplicity of mind. They could not visualise the dangers the patrol ran at sea.

This lack of co-ordination in carrying out a plan led to continual disappointments. Only in the few islands where the leader of the Andartes was a forceful man, able to stamp the impress of his character on the band, could they really be relied on.

Yet the Andartes could have played a vital part in the liberation, for they had all the advantages. Many of them were part-time irregulars, their normal civil life acting as a cover for their work. They could keep the Nazi Garrison under supervision without suspicion and any unusual movement, or the arrival of supplies, would be known immediately. Also, they knew all the goat tracks if they were hunted.

Finally, they could always rely on the other islanders to hide and feed them in emergency. Lack of discipline, and an agreed plan were their chief failings, combined with an intense individualism which sometimes made them refuse to join an attack because another man had planned it.

Eventually their continued demands for gifts of food and clothing wearied the civilians, who realised how little use the Andartes had made of their opportunities. In areas where civilians decided to restrict their help, the Andartes movement faded away.

It is not easy to discuss the political side of the irregular movement without making a single fact clear. A man who wanted arms to fight the Germans could, during much of the period, go only to ELAS to be supplied. Behind ELAS was EAM, the political side of the only movement which was on a national scale.

Colonel Zervas and the EDES movement were a tiny force in the background, distrusted by many for their alleged extreme Right Wing and Royalist opinions. Still more distrusted them because it was firmly stated that they helped the Germans against the Left-Wing irregulars in the same way as Mihailovitch and his Chetniks had done in Jugo-Slavia.

Charges of treason and "Quisling" activities kept them a minor force on the mainland, non-existent elsewhere, until the Christmas 1944 troubles. By this time Raiding Forces had long since ceased to rely on any promise of help from irregulars when planning an operation.

The men who joined ELAS to fight were of all political parties from centre to extreme left. Many of them neither knew or cared about the policy of EAM. After three years of Nazi occupation any Greek party was better than German dictatorship.

Appendix "C"

These were the Islands

In the course of their 381 raids and reconnaissance, on German held territory in the Aegean, the British and Greek troops of Raiding Forces visited not only the big, well-known islands, but scores of small ones, scarcely ever heard of outside their own immediate locality.

The following list of the seventy islands we landed on is complete. Most of them were visited more than once and frequently a reconnaissance patrol was rapidly followed by another to wreck the Nazi's installations:

DODECANESE		AEGEAN	
Leros	Archi	Samos	Phournoi
Levita	Pserimo	Mitilene	Khios
Symi	Plati	Lemnos	Psara
Galino	Telendos	Ikaria	Falconera
Pharmaco	Strongili	Samothrace	Kithera
Rhodes	Yalli	Thrassos	Crete
Kos	Pascia	Strati	
Patmo	Perigusa		
Lisso	Sirina		
Tilos	Alinnia		
Caidaro	Soskli		
Stampalia	Candelusia		
Calchi	Chinaro		
Nisyros	Cinousa		

TERROR BY NIGHT

CYCLADES		SPORADES
Mykonos	Siphnos	Skiathos
Syra	Ios	Jura
Naxos	Thira	Pelagos
Paros	Anafi	Skyros
Kimolos	Kea	Skopelos
Milos	Seriphos	Sfika
Amorgos	Folegandros	Iliodhromia
Denousa	Kythnos	
Kinaros	Delos	
Andros	Tinos	
	Yioura	
	Tinos	

Greek Sacred Squadron/Regiment Operations in the Agean Area

Samos (3 October to 19 November 1943)
Samos (7 to 18 March 1944)
Psara (29 to 31 March 1944)
Lesbos (3 to 4 April 1944)
Ios (26 to 27 April 1944)
Amorgos (28 to 29 April 1944)
Paros (2 to 5 May 1944)
Khios (6 May 1944)
Samos (15 to 24 May 1944)
Khios - Lagada village (9 to 15 June 1944)
Lesbos - Geras Bay, Mytilene (15 to 21 June 1944)
Kalymnos (30 June to 2 July 1944)
Symi (13 to 14 July 1944)
Karpathos (21 to 25 August 1944)
Santorini (27 August 1944)
Kos (7 to 8 September 1944)
Occupation and liberation of Khios (14 September 1944)
Occupation and liberation of Mykonos (25 to 28 September 1944)
Occupation and liberation of Samos (4 October 1944)
Involved in the liberation of Athens from the Germans (14 October 1944)
Occupation and liberation of Naxos (13 to 15 October 1944)
Occupation and liberation of Lemnos (16 to 17 October 1944)
Occupation and liberation of Milos (23 October 1944 to 9 May 1945)
Tilos (27 to 28 October 1944)
Nisyros (1 to 2 February 1945)
Tilos (1 March 1945)
Rhodes (1 to 2 May 1945)